Let's eat
raw

Dedication

This book is dedicated to those people who have sought and found a better way to live through the conscious food choices they make.

Acknowledgements

With thanks to my partner Clare Darwish for her patience and wonderful taste-testing skills. To Shambhala Farm for their continued support and the freshest and best fruit and vegetables. To Eclectic Style Noosa for supplying serving dishes for the photography. To the farmers and growers of Noosa Farmers Market for their continued dedication to bringing the best that the region can offer, week in and week out.

Let's eat
raw

recipes for improved health, energy and vitality

Scott Mathias

NEW
HOLLAND

Contents

About the Author

Scott Mathias is a digestive health specialist, RAW food educator and author. He says: My journey started at the age of nine, when my digestive system began 'rebelling' and I couldn't eat meat, wheat, dairy, processed foods and sugar. My body was unable to break down proteins properly so my body rejected them as soon as I ate; a symptom known as gastric reflux.

Almost half a century later I found a natural means to heal myself of what had by then become a life-long chronic digestive disorder.

I had been vegetarian on and off for most of my life because I found digesting meat to be difficult. I'd grown up with meat on the daily menu and eating it became a very painful experience. Back in the 1950s and '60s, when I was growing up, not eating meat was considered weird. My family doctor had no idea of the link between meat protein and my stomach's inability to break it down. Not surprisingly at an early age I began to doubt mainstream medicine. I also found that doctors generally were predisposed to look at the symptoms I suffered and treat those rather than find the cause of my ill health. Visits to a naturopath also proved unsuccessful.

The catalyst to my finding a solution to my ill health was two 'near-death' experiences. On both occasions, during my sleep, the contents of my stomach flowed into my lungs. Each time I dreamt that I was choking, and thankfully woke myself up.

While researching online, I read about the proteolytic (protein hungry) nature of the enzyme papain, which is derived from green papaya. I tracked some down, in its dried form, and began using it. The first night I took a level teaspoon dissolved in water I was able to lie completely flat for the first time in years and without a bout of reflux or discomfort. With prolonged daily use of the green papaya my symptoms began to disappear. Papain seemed to make my gut muscle stronger and less prone to the influences of poor food. I felt more and more comfortable in my stomach and knew I was onto something.

Being in and out of depression hadn't helped my healing either, though somehow I knew that a lack of nutrients in my system perpetuated my mental health issues.

I researched what a RAW food lifestyle might look like. I already had a comfortable relationship with fruit and vegetables, then several years ago I decided to commit to a 100 per cent RAW plant-based lifestyle. I chose to replace my old nutritional habits based on meat, wheat, dairy, processed foods and sugar and 'refresh' my cellular body each day with a diet that is rich in healthy phytonutrients. I removed from my pantry any foodstuffs that weren't 'alive', meaning all wheat, dairy and processed foods, and threw the lot out. In their place I worked out a new diet formula that I could be comfortable eating based on my research.

I found that there are a lot of RAW food zealots, whose views on what to eat or not to eat seemed extreme to me, so I tempered the information they shared with my own pragmatic views. I wanted my new lifestyle to be 100 per cent comfortable to maintain. I found that my new eating habits did not have to be difficult to put into practice just because I was choosing NOT to eat from troublesome food categories and neither did it have to be difficult to source the foods I chose to eat.

In the process of converting to a RAW food diet, I lost 3 stones 10 lbs (24 kilograms). I began to feel lighter in body and spirit. Since making that profound choice my life has changed radically. I no longer have an aching gut, and my body is nurtured with nutrients. I feel rejuvenated and alive. Now, more than 60 years in age, I actually feel much younger than my years. I have a spring in my step, just as I did at high school when I was a sports champion. I've noticed that many of my colleagues and peers are slowing down. In contrast, I feel ready to take on new challenges with renewed energy.

I choose not to take any dietary supplements or medication and since I changed my diet I no longer need to use green papaya powder. Instead I eat fresh plant-based nutrients daily to feed every cell in my body. This means that I receive all the nutrients my body needs predominantly from fruit, vegetables, nuts, seeds and sprouted grains. I am testament to my own choices. I like what I know and I love what I have become.

As a result of my own healing experience I founded iLifeFoods (Intelligent Life Foods) Pty Ltd, a digestive health and plant protein company. I now source 100 per cent pesticide-free green papaya powder, selling it through my local Noosa Farmers Market and online through my website scottmathiasraw.com. I also created a dehydrated beetroot, carrot, kale, Davidson's plum (*Davidsonia jerseyana*) and mango product called VegeShots, which is high in enzymes and naturally occurring antioxidants. After I had healed myself, I recall wondering to myself, 'Where to from here?'

I now devote my time to helping people identify the cause of their own chronic issues and provide recommendations based on my own healing experience. I studied Integrative Nutrition

to enhance my own understanding and use my knowledge every day.

I also use my food knowledge to prepare some of the tastiest food I have ever had the privilege to take into my body, including beautifully prepared fruits and vegetables, capturing the sweet, sour, salty, crunchy and creamy attributes of locally grown or sourced produce.

I conduct transformational RAW food masterclasses, teaching people how to transition or 'progress' with their RAW food lifestyle. Each month I open my home to a dozen guests and I prepare a seven-course RAW food meal for them, showing them each step of the recipe preparation process. They leave with a copy of my book *Understanding The Divine Gut – How to Eat Your Way Back To Ultimate Digestive Health*, a handful of easy-to-prepare recipes to try at home, and an eating experience that has been described as both 'sublime and zingy'.

I guess I am an authority on virtually every aspect of the digestive system; a result of my personal experiences as well as my in-depth research. You are most welcome to read more about what I have discovered on my blog (which can be accessed via my website). You can also see my range of iLifeFoods there too.

Each weekend at my beloved farmers market I meet people with the same or similar problems to those I once experienced. The questions they ask are the same as those I asked 10 years ago. 'How do I improve my own health?' My answer is simple. 'Use the food you put into your body as your healing tool'.

What is a RAW Food Diet?

There are no rules saying we should cook food or eat meat. What we eat is all about personal preference.

RAW food means any plant food such as fruit or vegetables, including sea vegetables such as wakame or dulse, as well as nuts and oils. Eating a RAW food diet literally means that the food that you choose to put in your body is not cooked in any way. When you eat RAW plant-based food, your body receives 100 per cent of the nutrients in the fruit and vegetables. Those nutrients ultimately enter the blood stream and I believe that the quality of my blood determines the healthy efficiency of my body – plain and simple.

When food is cooked, its structure is changed. The intermolecular bonds break down causing it to lose texture, colour and nutritional value. Proteins begin to be less effective and beneficial to the body. Carbohydrates (natural sugars) are leached away and flavours dissipate – the smell of food cooking is, in fact, the flavour compounds being released into the air by the cooking process. Much of your food's nutrients are therefore lost or compromised when cooked.

Most of the enzymes present in foods are destroyed at temperatures as low as 115°F (42.5°C). These food enzymes aid the digestive process and become active the moment food enters the mouth (the initial digestive process begins when we chew food). Eating enzyme-depleted food causes the digestive function to 'stall' and may create a state of trauma as well as reflux, bloating, indigestion and heartburn. In general RAW food is much easier to digest, passing through the digestive tract in half to a third of the time it takes for cooked food to make the same transition[1].

My best advice if you wish to begin adopting a RAW food diet is to introduce more plant-based nutrients gradually into your diet, working with a practitioner to help your gut work at optimum efficiency. Simply by introducing 50 per cent more plant-based nutrients into each day's diet will have a positive impact on the way your body operates and how you feel. When your gut begins to function properly your body will start to demand concentrated nutrients. The age-old wisdom utterd by Hippocrates, the father of modern medicine, 'Let food be thy medicine – medicine be thy food' is true. I healed myself as a result of the food I began to eat.

So what is the difference between a RAW vegan, a vegan and a vegetarian?

A RAW vegan will only eat whole 'live' food such as vegetables (including seaweeds), fruits, nuts and naturally occurring oils and sweeteners. There are no animal products in a RAW vegan's diet. The diet also lacks processed foods and sugars, an extension of the desire to remain healthy and free of 'dead'

[1]International Agency for Research on Cancer (1993). Some naturally occurring substances: Food items and constituents, heterocyclic aromatic amines and mycotoxins (International Agency for Research on Cancer, Lyon, France).Gold, L. S., Slone, T. H., Stern, B. R., Manley, N. B. & Ames, B. N. (1992) Science 258, 261-265.

or 'non life-supporting' foods. A RAW vegan tends to make and prepare all his or her meals from scratch enabling a connection to be made between the integral life force of the food and the body's desire to live. A RAW vegan will not consume bee products such as honey because it is considered an animal product.

For the purposes of eating a RAW food diet, food can be warmed or dehydrated at a temperature of no more than 115°F (42.5°C). After this the value to your body diminishes. No meal is cooked but some foods such as fruit, vegetables, seed breads (gluten-free), wraps, tortillas and flat bread can be dehydrated.

A RAW food vegan eats primarily plant-based nutrients including high protein greens such as kale, hemp seeds and nuts. Acceptable sweeteners include agave or coconut palm nectar syrup. With a RAW food diet, the palate responds to the nutritional purity of the fruit and vegetables without compromising quality as a result of cooking. You may feel full very quickly.

A vegan, on the other hand, does not eat any animal products but does eat cooked food.

A vegetarian eats cooked and uncooked vegetables, eggs, wheat, bee products and pasta and rice.

Some people make the transition to a vegan or RAW vegan lifestyle because of a need to overcome health issues. Others may also choose not to eat animal products for philosophical reasons – they choose to bring no harm to animals or they choose to ensure that no animal or living creature has been used for purposes of profit. My own steps toward a vegan lifestyle were health related though I now find it abhorrent that an animal should die for my culinary pleasure.

The benefits of eating a RAW food diet include:
- Increased energy levels
- No aches or pains
- Better sleeping patterns
- More bowel regularity
- No feelings of toxicity such as sore muscles and swollen joints. (Lethargy is often associated with toxicity along with a stale taste in the mouth, a white tongue and sallowness in the skin.)
- Higher levels of blood alkalinity. The ratio in a healthy body is 80 per cent alkalinity to 20 per cent acid. The higher the continual levels of acidity in the body, the greater the risk or presence of chronic illness. It is handy to have a roll of litmus paper (from a pharmacy) to do your own testing. Testing daily helps keep a check on levels of acidity. On most packs of litmus paper there is a colour legend that shows the levels of alkalinity or acidity depending on the colour of the paper after it has been immersed in urine or saliva. I used to test myself regularly out of sheer fascination but now I can simply tell what my levels approximate by how I feel. The more RAW plant-based foods you eat the higher the levels of alkalinity in your body. Bugs and bacteria enjoy an acid environment and find it difficult to survive in alkalinity.

Other advantages include:
- The cessation of flu and colds
- Weight stabilization (a balanced BMI – Body Mass Index)
- The emergence of beautiful skin
- More joyfulness
- A greater conscious sense of purpose and wellbeing
- NO medication whatsoever
- NO age-related illnesses. At my age the medical fraternity assume I will be suffering from increased blood pressure, perhaps pre-diabetes and increased PSA (prostate-specific antigen) levels. Because I eat and live the way I do I know more about my body than any medical practitioner could hypothesise. I don't buy into that system of beliefs.

• NO supplements, only compliments.

When I became a RAW vegan my foremost concern was where I would find suitable recipes. I later realised that the secret to finding a balanced RAW vegan lifestyle is about access to seasonally fresh vegetables and fruit. Without good quality fresh RAW materials to work with, this lifestyle choice is challenging.

I buy my week's supply of fresh fruit and vegetables at my local market without thinking too much about how I will prepare them. I buy what the season provides, which allows my body to remain in harmony with the produce that the Earth provides for me. Almost 99 percent of all the food I consume is sourced locally. I am lucky and live in an abundant area. I literally eat from the land I walk on.

Organic produce carries a premium and if you shop at a supermarket, demand it. It is better to pay more for healthier fruit and vegetables. See this as an investment in your health. I do.

I store produce chilled until I use it. This is largely dictated by the warm tropical climate I live in, but in colder climates it's OK to store products in a cool dark place. Separating fruit from vegetables is the ideal and as I do not have any meat or dairy products in my refrigerator I have extra space to utilise for storage. As I have said, I buy almost all of my food produce from my Sunday market. I only buy spray-free produce. I know the people who grow my food and know that they farm using organic methods.

ALL of the protein that I eat comes from vegetables. Kale, in particular, is known as the 'beef of the plant world' with up to eight times more protein than cow meat. Hemp products are powerhouses of nutrition with as much as 50 per cent protein in its nutritional make up. Hemp is rich in omega 3, 6 and 9 as well as amino acids and trace minerals. I enjoy it daily on my breakfast fruit salad. It is now recognised globally as the 'future of world food'.

I eat RAW nuts, using them to make milk and as a base for mayonnaise and sauces. RAW cashews are full of the essential amino acid L-tryptophan, which aids in the production of serotonin, the happy chemical. Ironically, I found out in my research that the absence of serotonin leads to depression. Where is it made? In the gut. So, if your gut is not functioning properly then the chances of suffering depression are increased. I can attest to that.

I eat lots of macadamia nuts too, sourcing 'fines', the course powder, made from nut pieces that are the result of the hulling process. Macadamias are sweet and rich in 'good fats'. They are a rich source of vitamin A, iron, protein, thiamin, riboflavin, niacin and folate. They also contain moderate amounts of zinc, copper, calcium, phosphorus, potassium and magnesium. Macadamia contains antioxidants such as polyphenols, amino acids, flavones and selenium and are a good source of carbohydrates such as sucrose, fructose, glucose, maltose and some starch-based carbohydrates. In other words they're a complete all-rounder in the nutritional stakes. You won't get the same nutritional benefits from roasted nuts, though.

Wouldn't you like to obtain and maintain excellent health? I did and the choice is yours. I now eat 20 per cent less food by volume than I did a few years ago and that decision has allowed my body to feel less stress. I sleep better providing more time for my body to repair itself.

Getting everything I need from the food I eat means I never have cravings. Food cravings are a big problem for some people but let me assure you that when your digestive metabolism is running well, and you eat cleanly, cravings will disappear.

Being in control of my health by using my own powers of nutritional discernment is a very empowering experience. When I wake each day with no aches or pains (I used to wake with swollen and sore ankles) then I know I am doing something right. The opportunity to live like this is available for everyone to enjoy.

Essential Equipment

In order to make the process of preparing the food you are about to eat a pleasurable experience you'll find the following equipment and kitchen aids useful:

Natural Wood Chopping Block
I have several natural wood chopping blocks made from recycled camphor laurel. Using recycled timber is a great way to give something back to the environment.

Dehydrator
This is perhaps the most expensive item on the equipment list but well worth the investment. I use mine almost daily. It's literally a square box with fans in the back and holds a series of trays one stacked above the other, upon which RAW food is placed for drying. (as in the picture below), or a smaller round version. I use mine to make my seed and flat breads

as well as to dry fruit and vegetables from time to time. I splashed out and bought a 9-tray model. The more heavy duty the machine, the longer it will last and the more reliable it will be.

Is it necessary to have a dehydrator? The short answer is no. You may use your oven to achieve a similar outcome. Simply set your oven at 42.5°C (122°F) or until the light comes on, activate the fan and open the door. Moisture will evaporate from the food but note that the drying time is halved when using an oven so REMEMBER to halve the time given in the recipes.

The longer you dehydrate food the longer it will keep.

Hand Blender and Food Processor
I use a powerful food blender, which is strong and durable and easy to clean and use it to make all sorts of dishes from ice cream to simple sauces. Run blenders at high speed for a minute or two to warm soup; the friction creates the heat.

I also have a food processor. It's a double-S blade domestic model with a heavy base. It has a pulse function, which is handy when preparing 'rice' dishes. A processor is wonderful for breaking down fruit and vegetable ingredients.

For smaller portions of liquids I prefer to use a personal blender. This is a smaller-scale blender. Look for one with a large blade for making sauces and smoothies and a small flat blade for powders and coffee beans.

Teflex Paper
Teflex is a heatproof plastic and is used as a vehicle

for holding foods while in the dehydrator. I use teflex for all my seed breads. If you cannot find teflex, or are not happy using it, then baking paper is acceptable.

Knives
When it comes to knives buy the best quality that you can afford. Finely honed stainless steel retains its edge well and can be sharpened easily. Don't forget to purchase a sharpener as well. Maintaining your knives makes life easier.

Spiraliser or Spirelli
A handheld or kitchen bench top model is fabulous for making vegetable spaghetti, angel hair spaghetti and other varieties of spaghetti. Made of durable plastic, it also has three different blades.

Food Form
This is a round stainless steel template a bit like a cookie cutter, used to present food attractively. Put it on a plate and stack food inside it. Remove the form and the food stack will stay in place.

Nut Bag
A specially designed 'sock-like' bag through which nut milk is poured, while held over a bowl, in order to gather the pulp after blending nuts. You could use a clean stocking or a piece of muslin to strain the liquid and retains the pulp or nut pieces. The nut bag can also be used to ferment nut cheeses.

Essential Ingredients

Agar Agar
This edible sea vegetable gelatine is available from health food shops and used to firm RAW food in a mould. Nutritionally good, it contains a beneficial balance of trace minerals.

Agave
Has become a popular sweetener and a natural alternative to processed white sugar or high-fructose corn syrup. It is derived from the blue agave (*Agave tequilana* and Agave *salmiana*) cacti plants. It has a glycaemic index (GI) of approximately 30 (In comparison white refined sugar has a GI of 60). Always look for a certified organic agave from a reputable brand.

Almond and Other Nut Flours
Place either dried activated or un-activated almonds into a smaller blender bowl and fit a small flat blade to your blender. Pulse until a powdery consistency is reached. All nuts can be turned to flour using this approach. The key is to ensure the nuts are very dry.

Organic coconut flour is made from fresh organic coconut flesh. It is a low carbohydrate, high-fibre, gluten-free alternative to wheat flour. If you have access to fresh coconuts then you can dry the white flesh from their insides in a dehydrator until 100 per cent dry, then grind in the small cup of a personal blender to make rice flour. You may also find coconut flour at a organic dry goods store.

Almond Nut Pulp
The by-product of the milk-making process and can be dried into a flour or made into a cheese.

Apple Cider Vinegar (ACV)
Find a brand of apple cider vinegar that hasn't been filtered or pasteurised. The process of pasteurisation removes some of the nutrients.

Banana Pepper
(Also known as the yellow wax pepper or banana chilli) is a medium-sized member of the chilli pepper family that has a mild, tangy taste.

Barley Miso
White barley miso is made from straight fermented soy beans and can be used in condiments such as mayonnaise, salad dressings or light sauces. The darker version is fermented barley. Both taste very salty. You may also find a fermented organic soy-based miso, which can be used for flavouring dishes.

Buckwheat
Despite its name buckwheat is actually a seed, sometimes known as a groat, and is a member of the dock family. It's starch-based and ideal as a breakfast cereal and for use as a flour in RAW breads. For activated buckwheat simply soak a cup in water overnight. By soaking the seed an enzyme inhibitor is released or activated. Next morning drain off the water and place the seeds into a nut bag and suspend in a sieve. Refresh with clean water three times a day and keep in a warm place. After about the third or fourth day the seed will start to sprout.

I tend to soak a couple of cups of buckwheat groats or seeds overnight and then arrange them in my dehydrator to dry for 3-4 hours. Stir every hour to ensure all the water is thoroughly dried off. What's left is a crunchy cereal-type seed, which I use on my fruit salad. I make my own flour by blending the groats. I never buy flakes.

Cacao and Cacao Nibs

Cacao pods are a fruit that grow on the *Theobroma Cacao* tree. Inside the pods are small brown cacao beans and it is from these that cacao powder come. Small nibs or pieces of bean are a by-product of the cacao production process; the rest of the bean is crushed for the powder.

Carob

Carob comes from the carob tree (*Ceratonia siliqua*), an evergreen native to the Mediterranean. The tree bears fruit known as carob pods. Carob has been used as food in the Jewish tradition for more

Below: Cacao

than 5000 years. It's a great alternative if cacao is not available.

Chokos

The round 'grenade like' vegetable are a tasteless, yet wholesome, vegetable. Chokos respond well to flavouring; a great alernative to zucchini (courgettes).

Coconut Palm Nectar Crystals

The coconut flowers at certain times of the year and leaves a residue of beautiful syrup. This syrup is gathered up and dried by the sun to create sugar-like crystals. The syrup can also be collected and can be bought in its liquid form. It has a low GI (glycaemic index) of 35.

Cured Grape Leaves

These are obtainable from Turkish or Middle Eastern grocery stores and are always handy to have on hand. They are salt-cured vine leaves. Don't forget to remove their stalks when using to make filled dolmades.

Curry Powder

Making your own curry powder can be fun. If you'd like to have a go at making your own here is a simple and easy recipe for a basic mix:
Cumin should be about 20 per cent of the total mix by weight:
9 per cent chilli powder
9 per cent dried ginger powder
9 per cent coriander powder
9 per cent fennel powder
9 per cent fenugreek powder
9 per cent turmeric powder
9 per cent cinnamon powder
9 per cent cardamom powder
9 per cent black pepper powder
Use your kitchen scales to determine exact weights

and 'try and test' your own mixture. Some people like more or less chilli.

Desert Salt
I prefer not to eat ocean salt because of the possibility of high levels of contaminants it may contain. Desert salt, which I prefer, is rich in magnesium chloride, the most versatile easily absorbed member of the magnesium family.

Dulse Seaweed Flakes
Dulse and kelp are edible seaweeds that have been harvested for years for their high mineral content and nutritional value. Dulse, also known as sea lettuce flakes, Rhodymenia palmate or red dulse, is a type of red seaweed harvested along the waters of Canada and the Atlantic coast. The fronds may grow on shells or in tidal areas on rocks. It's widely consumed in Northern European countries and Canada. Kelp or wild Atlantic kombu (Laminaria longicruris) is another type of edible seaweed that belongs in the same family and is similar to Japanese kombu. Arame, kombu and wakame are all types of kelp. Soak in water for a few minutes to rehydrate them, then add to certain RAW food dishes. Always check the origin of the seaweed. I prefer products from the clearer waters of Canada and Iceland. I avoid sea products from Japan because of the potential for radiation contamination.

Flaxmeal
Flaxmeal is actually ground linseed. It is high in protein and is a great 'binder' for seed breads and flat breads. You can grind your own but you may choose to buy it already ground. It is usually sold in re-sealable foil bags, which means that once opened it is best kept in the freezer to stop it from going rancid.

Dulse seaweed flakes

Galangal
Galangal is a member of the ginger family, and is similar in appearance, with its knobbly root-like form. Its skin is reddish-brown in colour, and thicker than that of ginger, while its flesh is creamy-white. Galangal has a strong, fiery flavour, reminiscent of a mixture of ginger, pepper and sour lemon. Galangal is usually peeled then sliced or grated (shredded), and is used in curries and other Asian dishes.

Heirloom Tomatoes
Look out for varieties of tomatoes, which fall into the antique or heirloom category. Most varieties pre-1945 are considered heirloom. After World War II hybridisation overtook the traditional varieties and in the process appearance and plant yield became the prime motivators for growing tomatoes.
Varieties include:
Green Zebra
Cherokee Purple
Black Krim

Black Russian
Canistrino
Yellow Valencia

Hemp Seeds

Hulled hemp seeds from the *Cannabis sativa* plant are one of nature's true nutritional gifts. They contain high levels of the digestible protein called edestin and contain 10 essential amino acids. They are also rich in Omega-3, 6 and 9 as well as essential fatty acids. In this form hemp seeds are non-germinating yet fully digestible without soaking, unlike some other nuts and seeds. They are a wonderful plant protein alternative and hemp is recognised the world over for its versatile attributes.

Kelp Noodles

Kelp noodles are made from brown seaweed, sodium alginate, a salt derived from seaweed, and water. Kelp is an edible seaweed high in nutrients. High in iodine, kelp also contains more than 70 minerals, trace elements, enzymes, potassium, magnesium, calcium, iron and 21 amino acids. Kelp noodles are an alternative to wheat pasta. Always ensure the packet you buy has RAW stamped on the front.

Macadamia Oil

Macadamia oil is derived from the nut of the same name. It is a non-volatile oil expressed from the nut meat of the macadamia - *Macadamia integrifolia* tree. Macadamia oil contains approximately 60 per cent oleic acid, 19 per cent palmitoleic acid, 1-3 per cent linoleic acid and 1-2 per cent linolenic acid. Some varieties contain roughly equal omega 6 and omega 3. Although macadamia is cultivated in many different parts of the world, the oil's fatty acid profile is not greatly influenced by environmental factors. It is also very stable due to its low polyunsaturated fat content. I use mostly macadamia oil because the

nuts grow near where I live.

Matcha Green Tea

Green tea is one of 'the mothers' of plant antioxidants'. It is finely milled green tea powder and available under a variety of brand names.

Mesculin

Mesculin is traditionally a selection of young salad leaves, which might include mustard leaves.

Mustard (RAW)

Take mustard seeds and soak them overnight. Next day pour off the water and place in a high speed blender with a small amount of either macadamia or olive oil. Blend thoroughly until you have a 'seedy paste' consistency. Add salt to taste and store in a glass jar in the refrigerator. Add some lemon juice to flavour, if you like.

Mesculin

Nama Shoyu

In Japanese, nama means RAW, or unpasteurised and shoyu means soy sauce. Nama shoyu is RAW, unpasteurized soy sauce used in certain RAW food dishes. The shoyu contains living enzymes and beneficial organisms and is preferred among vegans because of its 'live status'.

Nutritional (Savoury) Yeast

Nutritional yeast is inactive yeast that is a favourite among vegans because of its unique flavour and similarity to cheese when added to foods. Nutritional yeast is also a good source of vitamin B12. It is derived from fermented barley.

Nuts

Unsalted RAW cashews, almonds and walnuts are all available from health food stores or the natural food section of a supermarket. Roasted or salted nuts are best eaten on their own. They will not make good milks. Nut Butter can be made from virtually

Psyllium husks

any nut using a food blender. Follow manufacturers instructions.

Olives

Cured olives are considered RAW and make a great snack anytime. Keep them in the refrigerator.

Pomegranate Juice/Syrup

Pomegranate juice is made from the fruit of the pomegranate. It is used in food preparation both as a fresh juice and as a concentrated syrup. The RAW juice is always preferred but as an alternative the syrup can be used. It is available from Middle Eastern grocers.

Psyllium Husks

Psyllium comes from a shrub-like herb called *Plantago ovata*, most commonly found in India though nowadays grown all over the world. The plants produce thousands of small, gel-coated seeds, from which psyllium husk is extracted. The dried husk, which sometimes become powder-like, can be used to bind RAW breads together.

Rain Plum Powder

Davidson's plum (*Davidsonia jerseyanna*) is a tart and flavoursome red plum grown behind Northern New South Wales, Byron Bay. While there are other varieties, this variety is renowned for its high level of antioxidants called anthocyanins.

Rice syrup

This low GI sweetener, derived from rice, is ok to use if plant-based sweeteners are unavailable. It is very rich in taste so you would use very small quantities of this sweetener.

Seeds

Sunflower seeds are available from health food shops or the natural food section of a supermarket.

Pomegranate

Sumac Powder
Sumac is a spice, used mostly in Middle Eastern cooking, that has a lovely tart mild lemon flavour. The deep red berries are most often used ground into a powder. Available from Middle Eastern grocers.

Wakame
Wakame is a coarse edible brown seaweed used in Japanese cooking. When used RAW it is advisable to rehydrate it by soaking it thoroughly first. It is rich in trace minerals and imparts a 'strong seaweed' taste to RAW dishes.

Hemp seeds can be purchased online.

Shoyu Sauce
See Nama Shoyu

Sprouted Chickpeas
Using sprouted dried products is always preferable to using canned products. A can is a last resort because the product has been cooked . Sprouting is easy. Soak 1 cup of organic whole chickpeas over night. Next day, drain and rinse then place in a nut bag or sieve. Cover and leave on the bench top or place in a warm environment, such as a linen cupboard. After 3–5 days you will start to see little white tails emerge from the end of the chickpea. Continue to rinse them each day and after about a week or so (depending on humidity levels) your will have fully 'alive' chickpeas. Sometimes they are available already 'spouted'.

Milk and Bread

This chapter provides you with the skills and understanding needed to make your own gluten-free bread and lactose-free milk. Bread and milk are comfort foods and if you have digestive issues then these alternatives to traditional products will be kinder on your gut.

Nut Milk

Most nuts can be made into milk that has a creamy consistency. I enjoy the taste of nut milks, which are deliciously rich and almost sweet. However, I don't drink a whole a glass full of nut milk in one hit. Instead, I tend to use smaller amounts on my fruit salad in the morning or as the base for mayonnaises or sauces.

Hemp seeds are extremely nutritious too as they have a sweet nutty flavour. You can vary the volume of water that you add to the nuts and seeds according to the texture that you like.

1–2 cups (4–8 oz/115–225 g) whole nuts of your choice. Mixing nuts is not advisable because each has minor taste differences.

Water (Tap water is not recommended for use in RAW food preparation because of the likelihood of chemical contaminants. Use filtered.)

Put the nuts in a glass bowl, cover with water and leave overnight, allowing the nuts to soften and release the enzyme inhibitor.

Next morning, pour off the water and put the nuts into a blender. Add 2–3 cups (16–22 fl oz/475–750 ml) of clean water to the nuts (the ratio is 1 of nuts:2 of water, for example 9 oz (250 g) of nuts to 17.5 fl oz (500 ml). Pulse slowly then increase the speed and let run for 1 minute. Let stand for a few minutes then pulse again at full speed for 30 seconds.

Pour the liquid through a nut bag set over a large jug (pitcher). Thoroughly squeeze out all of the liquid and pour into a clean bottle. Keep refrigerated. Cashew milk will last for up to 7 days but almond milk will last only 3–4 days. I tend to make it as needed and use within a day or so.

TIP: The remaining nut pulp can be used to make 'cheese', as the base for creamy mayo, or for RAW desserts.

Buckwheat and Tropical Fruit Breakfast with Nut Milk

Buckwheat is a great alternative to cereal. It is rich in trace minerals including potassium, iron, vitamin B6 and magnesium, as well as dietary fibre. It has also been linked to lowering the risk of high cholesterol and high blood pressure. It is considered to be one of nature's 'miracle foods'.

¼ fresh pineapple (6 oz/175 g), chopped
2 oz (60 g) walnuts, chopped
½ cup (4 fl oz/120 ml) cashew or almond milk
1 cup (6 oz/175 g) buckwheat seeds, soaked overnight
   in water, rinsed and dried in a dehydrator for
   1 hour, or until crispy

2 oz (60 g) berries, puréed
2 tablespoons rice syrup, agave or maple syrup

Divide the chopped pineapple and walnuts between two bowls. Heap an equal amount of cracked buckwheat on top of each.

Pour on the nut milk, followed by the purée and then the syrup.

Serves 2

Sunny Seed Breads

This crunchy snack will keep for up to 10 days in an airtight container so is great to have to hand for when you need something to eat quickly. Add a dollop of avocado or nut butter, or top with sliced tomato and nut cheese.

2 cups (10 oz/280 g) sunflower seeds
1 red onion, diced
1 tomato, diced, or 4 sun-dried tomato halves, sliced
½ red bell pepper, diced
½ cup (4 fl oz/120 ml) water
1 cup (4½ oz/140 g) flaxseed meal (ground)

Add all of the ingredients, except for the flaxseed meal, to a blender or processor and blend until combined. Add the flaxseed meal and pulse the blender a few times to ensure the meal is fully incorporated.

Add just enough water to create a firm dough-like mixture.

Take one-third of the mixture and place onto heat resistant teflex paper. Cover with baking paper or another sheet of teflex, and using a rolling pin, roll out to a thickness of ¾ in (2 cm). Remove the covering paper and score the surface of the dough to the cracker dimensions you prefer. Repeat until the mixture is used up.

Place the trays in a dehydrator for 8–12 hours, turning the crackers after 3 hours and separating the pieces. They are ready when they are firm and crispy.

Makes up to 36 pieces of bread

Spicy Seed Crackers

Making seed bread follows a similar approach to the Sunny Seed Bread. These Spicy Seed Crackers are a delicious and crunchy alternative. Once you've made these a few times you could try adding different seeds.

2 cups (10 oz/280 g) sunflower seeds
½ cup (2½ oz/70 g) activated buckwheat
½ cup (2½ oz/70 g) flaxseed meal (ground)
½ cup (3/8 oz/10 g) dried, chopped dulse seaweed
¼ cup (½ oz/15 g) sun-dried or semi-dried tomatoes
   or bottled

¼ teaspoon red chilli, chopped
Cold water, just enough to form a dough
Salt and freshly ground black pepper, to taste

Add all of the ingredients to a blender or processor and blend until a malleable dough froms. Add extra water a little at a time, if required.

Take one-third of the mixture and centre on a sheet of teflex. Cover with another sheet, then roll out, with a rolling pin, to the thickness of a cracker. Remove the covering sheet. Score the dough with a knife to make cracker shapes. Repeat until the mixture is used up.

Dehydrate for 8–12 hours, turning every 3 hours and separating the snacks. They are ready when they are firm and crispy.

Makes up to 36 crackers or 3 trays

Sun-dried Tomato, Oregano and Garlic Breads

RAW bread? Yes absolutely. Once it's finished in the dehydrator or 'cool' oven you'll be surprised by just how good these taste too. When making, the thicker the bread the longer the drying time needed, so feel free to adapt the sizes to your own requirements. If you use an oven as your dehydrator halve the drying time.

1 cup (4¾ oz/130 g) zucchini (courgette), diced
1 tablespoon water
1 tablespoon lemon juice
2 garlic cloves
½ cup (1 oz/30 g) semi-dried tomatoes, chopped
4 dates, pits removed, soaked
1 cup (3½ oz/100 g) freshly ground almond flour
1 cup (3 oz/85 g) freshly ground buckwheat flour

1 cup (8 oz/225 g) psyllium seed husks
½ cup (2½ oz/70 g) flaxseed meal (ground)
1 teaspoon onion powder
2 teaspoons dried oregano
1 teaspoon sea salt

Combine the zucchini, water, lemon juice, garlic cloves, semi-dried tomatoes and dates in a blender and blend until smooth.

In a large bowl, combine the almond and buckwheat flours, psyllium husks, flaxseed meal, onion powder, oregano and salt. Add the zucchini mixture to the flour mixture and blend well using a wooden spoon.

Form into small flat breads or a thicker loaf as required. The bread will reduce in size by one-third through the drying process.

Dehydrate at 115°F (42.5°C) for 14 hours.

Keeps for up to 4 days in the refrigerator.

Corn and Tomato Naan Breads

I always keep some naan bread in an airtight container in the refrigerator. If friends drop around it means I have always something available to 'wrap' around other vegetables. Make these breads as thick or as thin as you like and experiment a few times until you get a desired consistency and shape.

3 cups (15 oz/420 g) frozen sweet corn kernels, thawed (frozen corn works better than fresh)
½ cup (2½ oz/70 g) flaxseed meal (ground)
½ cup (4 oz/115 g) psyllium husks
1 heaped teaspoon cumin powder
1 teaspoon desert salt

FOR THE TOMATO SAUCE
3 large tomatoes (12 oz/335g)
2 teaspoons semi- or sun-dried tomatoes
1 garlic clove
1 teaspoon onion powder
Freshly ground black pepper
Juice of 1 lime
Desert salt, to taste

To make the corn bread, thoroughly blend the corn, flaxseed meal, psyllium husks, cumin powder and salt in a food processor until the corn is completely broken down. Set aside.

To make the tomato sauce, blend all the ingredients in a blender, then add to the corn mixture and pulse until firm but rubbery. The mixture ideally will fall away from the sides of the blender.

Place a heaped dessertspoon onto a sheet of teflex or baking paper and, using a spatula, create a circle of the mixture ¼ in (5 mm) thick.

Place in the dehydrator for 4 hours at 115°F (42.5°C) turning halfway through. The bread is ready when it is pliable, firm and sponge-like.

Keep in an airtight container in the refrigerator for up to 1 week.

Olive Hemp Seed Crackers

This is a lovely Mediterranean variation of the Sunny Seed Bread and goes well with pesto or nut cheese.

3 cups (15 oz/420 g) sunflower seeds
½ cup (2½ oz/70 g) flaxseed meal (ground)
½ cup (1¾ oz/50 g) hemp seeds
½ cup (3 oz/85 g) kalamata olives, pitted and
    chopped
¼ cup (1½ oz/40 g) sun-dried tomatoes, chopped
Salt and freshly ground black pepper, to taste

Add all the ingredients to a processor or blender and blend until it forms a malleable dough. Add extra water a little at a time, if required.

Take one-third of the mixture and place on a sheet of teflex. Cover with another sheet, then roll out to the thickness of a cracker. Score into small squares with a knife. Repeat with the remaining mixture.

Place in a dehydrator and dehydrate for 8–12 hours, turning every 3 hours and separating the snacks. They are ready when they are firm and crispy.

Makes up to 36 crackers

RAW Zucchini and Corn Tortillas

Using corn in RAW food dishes is a great way to get nutrients and add colour into your food. I love Mexican-influenced food and I like my tortillas creamy. You can achieve this using the corn and skinless zucchini. The psyllium is the key to making a tortilla that can be folded and filled.

4 medium zucchini (courgettes), peeled
Sweet corn kernels from 2 corn cobs
½ cup (4 oz/115 g) psyllium husks
3 garlic cloves, crushed
2 teaspoons onion powder
1 tablespoon turmeric powder
¾ cup (3¾ oz/105 g) flaxseed meal (ground)

2 teaspoons desert salt
Freshly ground black pepper
2 cups (16 fl oz/500 ml) water

Blend the zucchini and corn kernels in a blender or food processor until smooth, then add the remaining ingredients, slowly drizzling the water into the mixture until it is a smooth spreadable consistency.

Spread a thin layer into tortilla shapes on teflex or baking paper, ensuring there are no gaps in the shape. Set the dehydrator to 115°F (42.5°C) (or oven to the lowest setting, fan on and door open, for 4–6 hours. Turn the shapes after about 2 hours. Take care not to over-dry them.

Store in an airtight bag in the refrigerator for up to 2 weeks or wrap, seal and freeze.

Serves 2

Tip: Fill with your favourite fillings such as salad, sliced avocado and mayonnaise. These tortillas are very versatile and great to have on hand.

Dips, Sauces and Snacks

Having a bowl of dip or a ready-made sauce always available in the refrigerator is such a handy thing. It means I have something to dip my seed bread into when I feel peckish. Add a good squeeze of lemon or lime juice to any dips or sauces that you store. The vitamin C in the juice preserves the nutritional goodness of the dip for a day or two.

Coconut and Coriander Raita

A lovely way to bring a 'creamy' dish into your RAW food day. This can be served with salads or served with one of the curries from the main courses section of this book.

1 x 14 oz (400 g) can coconut cream
½ fresh coconut or 1 cup (3 ½ oz/100 g) soaked dry
   shredded unsweetened (dessicated) coconut
1 cup (3½ oz/100 g) coriander (cilantro) , finely
   chopped, plus extra to garnish
1 garlic clove

1 green chilli
Juice of 2 limes
Salt and freshly ground black pepper, to taste

Put all of the ingredients in a blender and blend to a fine paste. Adjust the seasoning and serve in a bowl, garnished with coriander.

Sweet Tomato Cumin Relish

Serve this delicious relish with your favourite RAW food curry.

4 large Heirloom tomatoes, finely diced
½ red bell pepper (capsicum), finely diced
1 cup (6 oz/175 g) pineapple, diced
1 red onion, diced
1 heaped teaspoon cumin powder
¼ teaspoon fresh turmeric, chopped (dry is
    acceptable if fresh is unavailable)

¼ teaspoon root ginger, chopped
Small garlic clove, chopped
1 teaspoon coconut palm nectar sugar
Salt and freshly ground black pepper, to taste

Put all the ingredients in a blender and pulse to blend.

Refrigerate for a few hours to allow the flavours to meld.

Basil Pesto

This recipe can be made using basil or coriander. Basil is rich in trace minerals as well as vitamins A and C. In Asian countries it is often used as a tea to reduce inflammation. Use to top Sunny Seed Bread or as a RAW pasta accompaniment.

3 cups (15 oz/450 g) fresh basil leaves, stems removed
½ cup (2½ oz/75 g) pine nuts
½ cup (4 fl oz/125 ml) macadamia or olive oil
Salt and freshly ground black pepper, to taste

Place the basil leaves into the bowl of a food processor reserving a few for the garnish. Add the pine nuts and blend at high speed. Gradually add the oil a little at a time, until the mixture becomes runny but not flowing. Season to taste.

Decant into a container and store in the refrigerator.

Will last for up to 7 days.

Serves 2

Tomato Sauce

This tomato sauce is one of my refrigerator staples. It's quick to make and so is easy to have on hand. Try pouring it over zucchini fettuccine, or eat as a RAW cold tomato soup — delicious on a hot day.

2 large ripe tomatoes, quartered
½ red bell pepper (capsicum)
½ red onion
1 clove garlic
2 sun-dried tomatoes, halved
½ teaspoon mixed herbs
⅛ teaspoon of paprika

1 teaspoon of lime juice (acts as a sweetener and
   natural preservative)
Salt and freshly ground pepper, to taste

Add all the ingredients to the bowl of a blender or food processor and blend until creamy and smooth.

Serves 2 as a soup

Zucchini Hummus

This is a great oil-free version of the traditional hummus – easy and quick to make and just as tasty. It is also handy when you don't have chickpeas on hand. It can be served with seed bread, naan bread or as a salad 'side'.

1 large zucchini (courgette), approximately (6 oz/ 175 g), peeled and chopped
1 tablespoon tahini
1 tablespoon macadamia oil
½ red onion, chopped
1 teaspoon cumin
1 garlic clove

1 teaspoon of lime juice
⅛ teaspoon paprika
Salt and freshly ground black pepper, to taste
Sweet paprika, to garnish

Blend all the ingredients in a food processor. Place in a serving bowl. Garnish with a dash of sweet paprika.

Serves 2

Red Capsicum Dip

A zesty dip that can be whipped up in moments and served to hungry guests, or serve with some of your favourite greens and seed snacks.

FOR THE MARINADE
½ cup (4 fl oz/125 ml) macadamia or olive oil,
½ cup (4 fl oz/125 ml) apple cider vinegar
Juice of 2 limes or lemons
Salt and freshly ground black pepper, to taste

FOR THE CASHEW NUT CREAM
1 cup (6 oz/175 g) RAW cashews, soaked for 2–3 hours
2 medium garlic cloves
¼ cup (2 fl oz/60 ml) coconut milk or coconut cream
2–4 teaspoons nutritional (savoury) yeast
2 teaspoons lime or lemon juice
Salt and freshly ground black pepper, to taste

FOR THE DIP
1 large red bell pepper (capsicum), sliced and
 de-seeded
1 garlic clove
½ small red chilli
1–2 tablespoons Marinade (see recipe)
½ cup Cashew Nut Cream (see recipe)
2 tablespoons lime juice
1 spring onion (scallion), finely chopped
Salt and freshly ground black pepper, to taste

To make the marinade, mix the ingredients together in a bowl until combined.

To make the cashew nut cream, put all the ingredients in a food processor or blender and blend until smooth.

To make the dip, blend all the ingredients together until smooth. The dip will take on a delicate pink hue from the red bell pepper.

Serves 2

Vegetarian Taramasalata

I just love some of the Greek-style dips. When it comes to any RAW food dish requiring 'a taste of the sea' then I always add some soaked seaweed.

1 cup (6 oz/175 g) RAW cashews, soaked in water for
   3 hours in just enough water to cover the nuts
1 ripe avocado
½ onion
4 tablespoons macadamia oil
1 small strip wakame seaweed, soaked in water for
   30 minutes

Juice of 1½ lemons
½ small beetroot bulb, peeled
Salt and freshly ground black pepper, to taste

Place all the ingredients into a food processor and blend until smooth. Season to taste.

Serve with RAW vegetables such as carrot batons, celery sticks or cucumber slices.

Serves 2

Pickled Ginger

Making your own pickled ginger is simple — always keep it in a sealed jar in your refrigerator until needed. Use as an accompaniment to any RAW Japanese-style food.

1 cup (8 fl oz/250 ml) rice wine vinegar
¼ cup (2 fl oz/50 ml) water
2 teaspoons coconut palm nectar
1 large ginger root, peeled and thinly sliced

In a non-metallic bowl, mix the rice wine vinegar, water and coconut palm nectar.

Thoroughly immerse the ginger in the marinade. Refrigerate overnight to complete the curing process. Transfer to a storage jar. This will last several weeks.

Serves 2

RAW Garlic Mayo

Add some zing to your favourite salad ingredients with this delicious mayonnaise. This will keep for a week in the refrigerator in a sealed jar.

1 cup (6 oz/175 g) RAW cashew nuts, soaked
   overnight in water and drained
3 garlic cloves
Juice of 1 lime
2 teaspoons olive oil

½ teaspoon desert salt
Freshly ground black pepper, to taste
1 cup (8 fl oz/250 ml) water

Blend all the ingredients together in a food processor or blender, drizzling in the water until the mixture resembles the consistency of mayonnaise.

Serves 2

Sour 'Nut' Cream

Serving a 'sour' cream made from nuts is always a handy standby for those quick RAW meals or snacks. The savoury or nutritional (savoury) yeast imparts a delightful 'cheesiness' to the taste.

1 cup (6 oz/175 g) RAW cashew nuts, soaked in water
    for 3–4 hours and then drained
Juice of 2 limes
2 teaspoons nutritional (savoury) yeast
1 garlic clove
Salt and freshly ground black pepper, to taste

Blend all the ingredients in a bowl using a hand blender, until creamy. Adjust the seasoning, as required.

Serves 2

Chipotle Tomato Sauce

Chipotle is actually a smoked dried jalapeno – tasty and with a 'mild to hot' zing about it. It is used widely in Mexican dishes and works well with tomatoes.

2 large tomatoes
½ red bell pepper (capsicum)
½ cup (3 oz/85 g) semi-dried tomatoes
1 large spring onion (scallion)
2 garlic cloves
½ teaspoon chipotle or mild chilli powder
2 teaspoons olive oil

2 teaspoons lime juice
¼ cup chives, finely chopped
Salt and freshly ground black pepper, to taste

Blend all of the ingredients in a blender or food processor until smooth.

Serves 2

Moroccan Sunrise

The yellow summer squash has a slightly flattened top and scalloped edges. Both the skin and flesh are edible. It is an excellent source of vitamin C and contains dietary fibre. Make sure you select a shiny one. A squash that is dull in colour tends not to be fresh and crunchy.

2 teaspoons mild curry powder
Garlic Cashew Cream (see recipe)
Salt and freshly ground black pepper, to taste
1 medium yellow summer squash or large zucchini
    (courgette)

Blend the curry powder with the cashew nut cream. Season to taste.

Cut the squash or zucchini into thin slices using a mandolin or sharp knife.

Top each slice with a teaspoon of the cream to serve. You may also like to serve the sauce as 'dip' with squash or other vegetables such as sliced carrot or cucumber as dippers.

Serves 2

Pesto 'Magnifica' with Cashews, Basil and Kale

Not all pestos have to be made with basil. Try this version, made with kale, for a new dimension to the taste and texture of pesto. Kale is packed full of great vegetable protein.

1 cup (8 oz/225 g) cashew nut butter
¼ cup (2 fl oz/60 ml) olive oil
½ cup fresh basil
½ cup (3 oz/85 g) kale leaves, shredded
¼ teaspoon desert salt
2 garlic cloves, crushed
2 teaspoons onion, diced

2 teaspoons parsley, chopped
½ cup (3 oz/85 g) English spinach, shredded
Juice of 1 lemon

Blend all the ingredients together in a blender or food processor until thick and paste-like.

Serve on seed crackers, or use as a dip for thinly slice turnip, beetroot, cucumber or zucchini (courgette).

Store in a sealed container in the refrigerator.

Serves 2

Garlic Cashew Cream

This cream forms the basis for many other dips simply by adding different flavour combinations. The lime juice acts as a natural preservative.

1 cup (6 oz/175 g) RAW cashew nuts, soaked in water
    for 2–3 hours then drained
2 garlic cloves
¼ cup (2 fl oz/60 ml) Cashew Nut Milk (see recipe),
    coconut milk or coconut cream
2–4 teaspoons nutritional (savoury) yeast, according
    to taste preference

2 teaspoons lime juice
Salt and freshly ground black pepper, to taste

Blend all the ingredients together in a blender or food processor until smooth.

Store in an airtight container in the refrigerator for up to 10 days.

Serves 2

Baja Kale Chips

Kale chips are always a winner. They are packed full of nutrients and a wonderful alternative to standard potato crisps. They make a great RAW food snack.

1 large bunch curly-leafed kale – once the leaves are stripped, you will be left with approximately 1 lb (450 g)
½ pineapple, chopped
1 red bell pepper (capsicum), chopped

½ fresh red chilli, chopped
1 teaspoon salt

Remove the stalks, de-vein the kale and chop into bite-size pieces. Set aside.

In a blender or food processor, blend the pineapple, bell pepper, chilli and seasoning. Turn out into a bowl.

Add the kale to the bowl and, using your hands, thoroughly coat each with the pineapple and pepper mixture.

Spread the kale onto a sheet of teflex or baking paper, spreading the leaves out so that plenty of air can pass between the pieces. Place on trays in a dehydrator set at 115°F (42.5°C) or in a 'cool oven'. Dehydrate for 12 hours. For maximum drying efficiency I move the kale pieces around the tray every 2 hours. Adjust the drying time until the leaves are crispy.

Serves 2

Tip: Make sure the kale chips are crispy. They will store, though they will gather moisture after a few days and soften up. You can put them back in the dehydrator to make them crispy again.

Soups

I just love a soup created from entirely RAW ingredients. The recipes included in this chapter are comforting and delicious, perfect for any time of the year. RAW soups can be served cold, at room temperature or warmed in the dehydrator. The key is to ensure all the nutrients are kept intact; boiling a soup destroys much of the goodness.

Gazpacho

Quick, simple, tasty and wholesome is how I would describe this dish. Feel free to vary some of the ingredients based on what's available in your local area.

1 large tomato, plus extra to garnish
½ Lebanese cucumber
½ red bell pepper (capsicum), plus extra to garnish
1 spring onion (scallion), plus extra to garnish
2 teaspoons macadamia oil
¼ teaspoon paprika

2 teaspoons lime or lemon juice (add more if you
  want your soup to taste sweeter)
Salt and freshly ground black pepper, to taste

Blend all of the ingredients in either a blender or food processor until coarsely chopped and flowing.

Pour into a soup bowl and garnish with small cubes of tomato or bell pepper and spring onion. Serve with Sunny Seed Bread.

Serves 2

RAW 'Udon Noodle' Soup with Fennel and Ginger

There is nothing like bringing some Asian flavours into your cooking. The blend of spices and herbs add depth of flavour and heat.

1 cup (8 fl oz/250 ml) water
¼–½ red bell pepper (capsicum)
1 cup (8 fl oz/250 ml) Cashew Nut Milk (see recipe)
2 teaspoons white miso
½ in/1 cm piece root ginger, to taste
¼ teaspoon paprika
1 small garlic clove

¼ teaspoon turmeric
4 teaspoons lime juice
½ zucchini (courgette), peeled
Several slices of fennel
Chopped chives, to garnish
1 red chilli, chopped, to garnish
Salt and freshly ground black pepper, to taste

Add the water, bell pepper, cashew milk, miso, fresh ginger, paprika, garlic, turmeric and lime juice to the bowl of a blender or food processor. Blitz for 30 seconds. If you want warm soup then blend at full speed for 1 minute, or until the desired temperature.

Peel and discard the skin from the zucchini. Using a spiraliser make fine 'udon' style noodles with the flesh. Add these to the soup, placing the chopped fennel on the top along with some green chives and a chilli, to taste. Season, if necessary.

Serves 2

Warm Miso and Vegetable Soup

Another quick and easy soup, which can be served either warm or at room temperature. Miso adds an earthy, salty flavour to food. It is an excellent source of iron, calcium and B12 vitamins.

2 tablespoons white barley miso or any miso of choice
1 garlic clove
½ chilli, chopped
1 teaspoon root ginger, chopped
2 spring onions (scallions)
½ red bell pepper (capsicum), plus extra to garnish
2–3 cups (16–24 fl oz/500–750 ml) warm water

Salt and freshly ground black pepper, to taste
2–3 seasonal vegetables such as celery, cauliflower, broccoli or zucchini (courgette), diced
Green (French) beans, sliced, to garnish
1 teaspoon macadamia oil

Blend all the ingredients except for the seasonal vegetables and the oil with the blender set to high speed.

Divide between two serving bowls, then add the vegetables and the bell pepper.

Drizzle with macadamia oil.

Serves 2

Chocolate and Macadamia Nut Soup

This amazingly tasty and nourishing dish may be prepared as a main course or dessert. The beautiful thing about most sweet RAW food recipes, they can be eaten as a main course or as a dessert. In fact, in my household we don't differentiate at all. A word of caution though; this dish may be too rich for some people so serve small portions.

¾–1 cup (3–4 oz/85–115 g) macadamia nuts, crushed
2 teaspoons RAW cacao powder
1–2 cups (8–16 fl oz/250–500 ml) almond or cashew
    Nut Milk (see recipe)
2 teaspoons agave, to taste
Cacao nibs, to decorate

Blend all the ingredients in blender until a creamy consistency is achieved and divide equally between two bowls.

Serves 2

Creamy Miso Dulse Mushroom Soup

Dulse seaweed imparts a lovely flavour to this soup. Purchased as dehydrated flakes, the seaweed rehydrates the moment it is added to liquid. Leave the mixed ingredients to stand for 1 hour or so for the flavours to develop before serving.

3 cups (24 fl oz/750 ml) cashew or almond milk
2 tablespoons cashew nut pulp
4 large Swiss (Portobello) mushrooms
1 fl oz (30 ml) miso paste
1 teaspoon dried dulse seaweed flakes
Salt and freshly ground black pepper

1 teaspoon macadamia oil
2 medium Marinated Mushrooms, sliced (see recipe), to garnish

Put all the ingredients in a blender and blend at high speed, to create a foaming mixture, which is tepid to the touch. The longer you leave the blender running at high speed the warmer the mixture will become.

Divide between soup bowls and garnish by floating the marinated mushrooms on the surface. Season to taste and add a splash of macadamia oil around the edges.

Serves 2.

Tom Yum RAW Hot-and-Sour Thai Soup

The aromatic kaffir lime bush tree of Asian origin imparts the most exquisite flavours to everything it comes into contact with. You can buy the leaves dry from an Asian grocer, or if you have the right climate you could find yourself a kaffir lime tree to nurture.

4 kaffir lime leaves, torn with centre vein removed

1 tablespoon galangal, sliced thinly

6 coriander (cilantro) roots, plus 1 tablespoon fresh leaves, finely chopped

2 whole shallots, sliced

2 cups (16 fl oz/500 ml) warm water

6 red medium chillies, finely chopped

2 teaspoons Fish-like Sauce (see recipe)

Juice of 2 limes

1 tablespoons coconut palm nectar

1 tablespoon coconut milk

Salt and freshly ground black pepper, to taste

1 lemongrass stalk, cut into 1 in (2.5 cm) pieces and smashed with a heavy knife handle

8 cherry tomatoes, halved

½ cup (2 ½ oz/75 g) button (white) mushrooms, sliced

FOR THE FISH-LIKE SAUCE

¼ cup (⅜ oz/9 g) dulse seaweed flakes

Juice of 1½ limes

1 teaspoon desert salt

4 teaspoons agave or 1 teaspoon coconut palm nectar

½ red chilli

To make the fish-like sauce, add all the ingredients to a blender or food processor and blend until smooth. Set aside. This sauce will keep for several weeks in the refrigerator.

To make the soup, blend all the ingredients, except for the lemongrass, tomatoes, mushrooms and coriander leaves in a blender until smooth.

Divide the liquid between serving bowls then garnish with the lemongrass, tomatoes and mushrooms. Leave to stand for 30 minutes, then divide between the serving bowls.

Garnish with fresh coriander.

Serves 2

Starters

In a RAW lifestyle starters are light, tasty and quick-to-prepare snacks. Fruits, vegetables and breads presented with flavourful sauces tempt the tastebuds and whet the appetite.

Avocado 'Carpaccio' with Chilli-Lime Nut Sauce

A delightfully rich and nourishing dish made of avocados, which are packed with good fats. This dish can be served on its own or as an accompaniment to a main course.

1 firm, ready-to-eat avocado

FOR THE NUT SAUCE
¼ cup (2 fl oz/60 ml) cashew or almond milk
½ cup (1¾ oz/50 g) macadamia nuts, whole or pieces,
    soaked in water for 12 hours
2 teaspoons tahini
½ red bell pepper (capsicum), chopped, reserving a
    few pieces for a garnish

1 garlic clove
¼ teaspoon paprika
2 drops Tabasco chilli sauce or ½ red chilli, chopped
2 teaspoons lime juice, plus extra if needed
Salt and freshly ground black pepper, to taste
Parsley, to garnish

To make the nut sauce, blitz all the ingredients together in a blender. If the sauce is too thick, simply add more lime juice to 'lighten' it.

Leaving the skin on, remove the seed from the avocado. Gently scoop out the flesh and layer it neatly on a plate.

Pour the nut sauce over the avocado. Garnish with parsley sprigs or diced red bell pepper.

Serves 2

Spicy Guacamole

This old favourite is easy to prepare. I love to jazz mine up with extra herbs, which bring life to the lovely creamy consistency of the avocado. The guacamole keeps for a few days in the refrigerator: the lime juice acts as a natural preservative.

1 ripe avocado
½ red chilli
½ cup chopped cilantro/coriander or add extra fresh
   herbs (see below)
Juice of 1 lime, plus more if needed (the more you
   add the sweeter the dip will be)
¼ red onion, chopped

¼ teaspoon paprika
½ cup mixed fresh green herbs such as coriander
   (cilantro), parsley, thyme and oregano (optional)
Salt and freshly ground black pepper, to taste
Sunny Seed Bread (see recipe), to serve
Red bell pepper (capsicum), chopped, to serve

Place all the ingredients into the blender and pulse until it is a creamy and buttery consistency.

Add more lime to get the mix smoother if desired.

Apply liberally to Sunny Seed Bread, top with some red pepper.

Serves 2

Avocado Filled with Spicy Salsa

Need a meal that takes less than 5 minutes to prepare? Well this dish is the answer – it's a lovely and lively taste combination.

1 tomato
1 small red onion
½ Lebanese cucumber
½ green bell pepper (capsicum) or banana pepper
Juice of 1 lime
¼ teaspoon apple cider vinegar
¼ teaspoon macadamia oil

Freshly ground black pepper
1 avocado, halved and seed removed

Dice the tomato, red onion, cucumber and pepper and place in a mixing bowl.

Add the lime juice, the apple cider vinegar and the macadamia oil and season, to taste.

Scoop out a little more avocado flesh from each avocado half, place the avocado halves in a small serving dish or bowl and fill the cavities with the diced mixture. Grind some black pepper over the top.

Serves 2

Marinated Mushrooms Tapas Three Ways

Marinating vegetables is a great way to 'soften' them and gives the taste and appearance of being 'cooked'. Mushrooms respond well to marinade.

24 cured olives

FOR THE MARINATED MUSHROOMS
24 small button (white) mushrooms
½ cup (2 fl oz/60 ml) macadamia oil
½ teaspoon of lemon or lime juice
¼ teaspoon of apple cider vinegar
¼–½ cup (2–4 fl oz/60–120 ml) agave syrup

FOR THE TOMATO SALSA
1 large tomato
⅓ red bell pepper (capsicum)
⅓ Lebanese cucumber
⅓ habanero or a hot green pickled chilli
Juice of 1 lime or lemon
Few springs of coriander (cilantro)
4 teaspoons macadamia or olive oil
2 teaspoons apple cider vinegar
Salt and freshly ground black pepper, to taste

To make the marinated mushrooms, clean the mushrooms by wiping them with a damp cloth.

Put the mushrooms, macadamia oil, lime juice, agave syrup, apple cider vinegar and salt and pepper in a mixing bowl. Mix the mushrooms thoroughly through the marinade and set aside for 2 hours.

Refrigerate to marinate for 24 hours.

To make the tomato salsa, dice the tomato, red bell pepper, cucumber and habaneros and place in a bowl.

Add the lime juice, sprigs of coriander, the macadamia oil and apple cider vinegar to the salsa mix and stir through. Season with salt and pepper.

Serve some of the marinated mushrooms, the salsa and olives in three separate bowls as a starter to a main dish.

Serves 2

Two-Minute Salsa Salad and Nut Mayonnaise

The salsa is a great fall back when unexpected guests turn up. It's quick to make and great served with bread.

FOR THE NUT MAYONNAISE

½ cup (4 fl oz/125 ml) Cashew Nut Milk (see recipe) or coconut milk
½ cup (3 oz/85 g) chopped macadamia or cashew nuts, soaked overnight in just enough water to cover
2 teaspoons tahini
½ red bell pepper (capsicum), chopped
1 garlic clove
¼ teaspoon paprika
Salt and freshly ground black pepper, to taste
Fresh basil, to garnish

FOR THE SALSA

2 cups (12 oz/335 g) fresh or thawed frozen sweet corn kernels
1 red onion, sliced
8 cherry tomatoes, sliced in half
1 red bell pepper (capsicum), diced
1 red chilli, finely chopped
½ cup (2 oz/60 g) cauliflower florets
3 medium mushrooms, sliced
2 medium pickled gherkins, diced

To make the nut mayonnaise, put all the ingredients together in a blender or processor and blend until combined.

To make the salsa, mix the diced and prepared vegetables in a serving bowl with your fingers.

Add some of the nut mayonnaise and blend through. Place on a serving dish and garnish with fresh basil. Season with ground pepper and sea salt.

Serves 2

Cheesy Herb Tomato Boats

Vegetables that can be scooped out and filled with a tasty filling can be a fun way to present and eat RAW food. Tomatoes are ideal for this.

4 medium tomatoes, halved
2 cucumbers, finely diced
⅓ red bell pepper (capsicum)
¼ cup chopped chives
⅓ cup Cashew Nut Cream (see recipe) 2–3 teaspoons
    nutritional (savoury) yeast

2 teaspoons lime juice
Salt and freshly ground black pepper

Scoop out the tomato flesh from the tomato shells and set aside.

Dice the cucumber and bell pepper and mix together in a bowl. Add some chives, reserving a few for decoration.

Put a tablespoon of the creamy nut sauce in a small bowl and add the nutritional (savoury) yeast. Whisk together then add the lime juice. Season to taste.

Add the nut sauce to the diced vegetables and mix thoroughly.

Spoon the mixture into the tomato halves. Garnish with chives and a few grinds of cracked pepper.

Serves 2

Cherry Tomatoes in Basil Oil

This is a 'show stopper' dish because of the extreme green colour of the basil oil, which contrasts with the red of the tomatoes. The taste is sublime.

24 cherry or grape tomatoes, halved
4 spring onions (scallions), sliced
⅓ cup (1¾ oz/50 g) pine nuts.
Olive oil, for drizzling

FOR THE BASIL OIL
4 cups of fresh basil leaves
½ cup (4 fl oz/120 ml) olive oil
Small garlic clove (optional)
4 teaspoons lime juice
Salt and freshly ground black pepper, to taste

In a bowl mix the halved tomatoes, sliced spring onions and pine nuts.

To make the basil oil, add all the ingredients to the bowl of a blender or food processor and blend thoroughly until smooth. Decant into a serving bowl. Arrange the tomatoes, spring onions and pine nuts on top. Drizzle with some olive oil and add a grind of black pepper.

Serves 2

Main Courses

Eating RAW encourages you to eat with the seasons and to incorporate a broad range of vegetables into your diet. There are myriad combinations of vegetable, herb and spice dishes to try, each with delectable flavours and appealing textures.

Two-Minute Zucchini Fettuccine with Asparagus and Fresh Olives

This is a quick and easy meal in which you can use a spiraliser to create fettuccine-like zucchini pasta. It tastes sweet and juicy.

1 large firm zucchini (courgette)
3–4 asparagus spears
1 garlic clove, crushed
2 teaspoons macadamia or olive oil
6 fresh olives (stuffed or pitted)
Juice of 1 lime
Salt and freshly ground black pepper, to taste

Leaving the skin on, spiralise the zucchini into a large bowl.

Slice the asparagus into bite-sized pieces and add to the bowl with the crushed garlic.

Squeeze half the lime into the bowl and add a drizzle of macadamia or olive oil together with the olives. Season with salt and pepper. Toss the ingredients together before serving.

Serves 2

Mushrooms on 'Toast' with RAWlandaise Sauce

When I was young my mother cooked mushrooms in a pan with a knob of butter, some garlic and salt and pepper and would serve them to us on toast for breakfast. This is my RAW version of that dish.

1 avocado, halved, seed removed and flesh chopped
2 teaspoons nutritional (savoury) yeast
½ garlic clove, chopped
4 teaspoons lime juice
2 or 3 small Marinated Mushrooms (see recipe)
Sunny Seed Bread (see recipe), to serve
Salt and freshly ground black pepper, to taste

1 tablespoon parsley, chopped, to serve
¼ teaspoon paprika, to garnish

Blend the avocado, nutritional (savoury) yeast, garlic, lime juice and seasoning together until creamy.

Place the sunny seed bread on a plate and distribute the mushrooms on top. Spoon the creamy sauce on top of the mushrooms.

Season with salt and pepper. Top with chopped parsley and dust with paprika.

Serves 2

Avocado Cucumber Compress with Mushroom Medallions and Wasabi Nut Sauce

This is a great way to eat good fats and healthy proteins in one meal. The mushroom medallions are nutty and sweet and the wasabi nut sauce adds heat. A good RAW dinner party treat.

½ Lebanese cucumber
¼ red onion
2 teaspoons lime juice
1 ripe avocado
2 teaspoons apple cider vinegar
Salt and freshly ground black pepper, to taste
1 teaspoon chopped parsley or coriander (cilantro), to garnish
Green salad, to serve

FOR THE SAUCE
1 cup Cashew Nut Cream (see recipe)
¼ teaspoon fresh wasabi paste or paste from wasabi powder
¼ teaspoon desert salt, to taste
Green salad, to serve

Finely dice the cucumber and red onion and put in a bowl, add the lime juice and apple cider vinegar. Stir and set aside.

Peel, pit and coarsely chop the avocado flesh. Place in a bowl and break up with a fork to a chunky consistency.

Place a stainless steel food form onto a serving plate. Fill with a layer of the avocado, followed by a layer of the diced cucumber and onion, then a layer of avocado. Top with a layer of the diced vegetables. Press gently down on the contents of the form, then gently slide the form away.

Drizzle cashew nut cream over the top of the compressed stack. Serve with green salad.

Serves 2

Portobello Mushrooms Stuffed with Parmesan and Peppers

Portobello mushrooms are large and make useful containers to hold other flavoursome ingredients.

4 medium Portobello (Swiss brown) mushrooms
½ cup (4 fl oz/120 ml) olive oil
Juice of 2 limes
1 garlic clove, crushed
Salt and freshly ground black pepper, to taste
1 red bell pepper (capsicum), finely diced
1 red radish, finely diced
½ red onion, finely diced
¼ teaspoon fresh or dried thyme

½ teaspoon fresh or dried oregano
2 teaspoons Nut Parmesan Cheese (see recipe)
Salad, to serve (optional)

FOR THE NUT PARMESAN CHEESE
1 cup (4 oz/115 g) macadamia nuts
4 teaspoons nutritional (savoury) yeast
¼ teaspoon ground black pepper

To make the Nut Parmesan Cheese, crush the macadamia nuts to a coarse powder. Add the nutritional (savoury) yeast and thoroughly blend. Add the black pepper. Store in an airtight container in the refrigerator.

Wipe the mushrooms with damp kitchen paper. Remove the stalks.

In a bowl, mix the olive oil, lime juice, garlic, and salt and pepper. Immerse the mushrooms in the bowl and set aside for 1–2 hours until the mushrooms have absorbed the marinade.

Coarsely pulse the remaining ingredients, including the mushroom stalks, in a processor, adding a spoon or two of the mushroom marinade to the mixture.

Remove the mushrooms from the marinade and allow the excess moisture to soak off onto kitchen paper.

Spoon the blended vegetable filling into the mushroom cups and garnish with some of the remaining nut Parmesan. Serve as they are or with a salad.

Serves 2

Mushroom and Walnut 'Burgers' with Tomato Sauce

RAW means you can still enjoy the sweetness and succulence of a 'burger' but without the animal product. When served with a freshly made tomato sauce the taste sensation is extraordinarily satisfying.

2 large Swiss brown or Portobello mushrooms (the Swiss brown variety has a nuttier flavour)
¼ cup (1 oz/30 g) walnuts
¼ red onion, diced
Salt and freshly ground black pepper, to taste

Tomato Sauce (see recipe)
Sunny Seed Bread (see recipe)
Salad, to serve

Blend all the ingredients together in a food processor. Mix to a moist paste adding a little water if too dry, but being careful not to make the mix too wet, otherwise it won't form burger shapes.

Form the mixture into burger-like rounds or patties. Place into the dehydrator at 115°F (42.5°C), or in the fan oven at the lowest possible setting and leaving the door open. Turn every hour so that the exterior becomes firm. The burgers will need 3–4 hours to firm up plus another 3 hours.

Serve topped with Tomato Sauce and Sunny Seed Bread (see recipe) or with salad vegetables.

Serves 2

Tip: Store in an airtight container for up to 10 days.

Sweet Potato Pesto 'Linguine' with Sun-dried Tomatoes

RAW sweet potato, you ask? Yes, if it's been soaked in lime juice for an hour or two the acid in the lime breaks down the surface of the sweet potato and softens it ready for eating. Rich in trace minerals and vegetable fructose, this is a wholesome meal.

1 long narrow sweet potato, peeled
6–8 generous teaspoons Basil Pesto (see recipe)
¼ cup (1 oz/30 g) pine nuts
½ cup (3 oz/85 g) sun-dried or dehydrated cherry
    tomatoes
4 teaspoons lime juice
2 teaspoons macadamia oil

Salt and freshly ground black pepper, to taste

Spiralise the peeled sweet potato and steep in lime juice in a non-metallic bowl for 1–2 hours.

Add the basil pesto, pine nuts and chopped sun-dried tomatoes, mix together and transfer to a serving bowl. Drizzle over the macadamia oil and season with the sea salt and cracked pepper.

Serves 2

Tip: Dehydrated tomatoes can be purchased in a jar from health food stores. Alternatively, put small cherry tomatoes into a dehydrator or oven for 4–6 hours.

Lime-Infused Carrot and Cucumber with Porcini Mushrooms

This is a 'gourmet like' dish and is great as both a main course or a starter. The 'lime-infused' cucumber and carrot lifts these two humble vegetables into another dimension. The delicate earthiness of the mushroom adds a flavour to the creamy avocado, which is sublime.

7–9 pieces of dried porcini, Swiss brown or Portobello mushrooms
½ carrot, peeled
½ cucumber, peeled
Juice of 1 lime
½ avocado, puréed

Salt and freshly ground black pepper, to taste
2 teapoons macadamia oil

Soak half of the dried mushrooms in water for a few minutes until they are fully rehydrated.

Spiralise the carrot and cucumber into separate glass bowls and add lime juice to each. Mix through with your fingers and leave for an hour or so.

Using a coffee grinder attachment on a blender or food processor, grind the remaining dried mushroom pieces to a fine powder.

In a bowl, mix the avocado with the dried mushroom powder and a pinch of salt.

Position the large stainless steel food form on a serving plate. Wrap a layer of the infused spiralised carrot around the inside of the base followed by a layer of cucumber creating a bird's nest effect. Fill the centre with the avocado mushroom cream until it just comes over the top. Add a couple of pieces of the rehydrated mushrooms to the top. Remove the food form. Add a grind of cracked pepper and a splash of macadamia oil to finish.

Serves 2

RAW Risotto

This is a vegetable 'take' on rice risotto. RAW foodies replace traditional rice with vegetables such as cauliflower, turnip or parsnip. The 'rice' can be achieved by processing the vegetable. Serve as a main or a starter.

½ turnip or parsnip, finely diced
4 large cauliflower, cut into small florets
1 medium red bell pepper (capsicum)
½ spring onion (scallion)
Salt and freshly ground black pepper, to taste
1 cup Cashew Nut Cream (see recipe)

Chives, to garnish
Freshly ground black pepper

Dice all the vegetables, except for half of the bell pepper.

Put the nut cream into the blender with the remaining bell pepper half. Blitz thoroughly to create a red/orange sauce.

On a serving plate, place the vegetables in a neat mound and pour over the sauce. The tip is not to make your vegetables pieces too large. Garnish with chives and some freshly ground pepper.

Serves 2

Fennel, Bean and Sun-dried Tomatoes with Hemp Seeds

Fennel is a vegetable you either love or hate. Its aniseed fragrance and taste is quite defined. Fennel is a great blood cleanser with wonderful antioxidant characteristics. It is great served as an accompaniment to other RAW dishes.

1 lb 2 oz/500 g fresh green (French) beans, sliced
   diagonally into bite-sized pieces
1 fennel bulb, julienned
¼ red onion, chopped
½ cup (3 oz/85 g) sun-dried or cherry tomatoes
½ cup chopped fresh broad leaf parsley
2 teaspoons macadamia oil

2 teaspoons apple cider vinegar
2 teaspoons lime or lemon juice
Salt and freshly ground black pepper, to taste

Put the prepared beans, fennel and onion into a bowl. Add the sun-dried tomatoes and finely chopped parsley followed by the oil, apple cider vinegar and lime juice. Season and blend with your hands.

Serves 2

Purple Cabbage Rounds with Apple and Walnut Filling

The sweet characteristics of the apple merging with the walnut and the crunchiness of the red cabbage makes for a great snack or main course. The purples of the cabbage contain anthocyanin antioxidants so its not only a good looking plate but also a healthy one.

1 small red or purple cabbage
2 teaspoons lime juice
2 teaspoons apple cider vinegar
2 teaspoons macadamia oil
1 small apple
2 teaspoons walnuts, chopped

Salt and freshly ground black pepper, to taste
Chives, to garnish

Slice the cabbage into thin rounds. Set aside in a bowl with the lime juice, apple cider vinegar and macadamia oil.

Dice the apple, with skin on, and chop the walnuts.

On a serving plate, take some cabbage and begin to fill a stainless steel form leaving a hollow centre. Fill the hollow with the walnut and apple mix. Remove the form. Pour some of the remaining liquid over the top.

Season to taste and garnish with chives.

Serves 2

Thai Kelp Noodles with Sweet-and-Sour Sauce

If you love the flavours of Thailand there's no reason to go without while enjoying a RAW food lifestyle. I often use kelp noodles, which are available from Asian food stores or online. They are wheat- and egg-free.

1 packet (12 oz/335 g) kelp noodles
¼ red bell pepper (capsicum), finely diced
4 spring onions (scallions), sliced
¼ cup Marinated Mushrooms (see recipe), chopped
Salt and freshly ground black pepper, to taste
2 tomatoes, to serve
Green vegetables, sliced, to serve
Lime juice, to serve
Macadamia oil, to serve

FOR THE SWEET-AND-SOUR SAUCE
1 tablespoon macadamia oil
Juice of 1 lime
2 teaspoons coriander (cilantro), finely chopped
2 tablespoons apple cider vinegar
1 garlic clove, finally chopped
½ chilli, finely chopped
Salt and freshly ground black pepper, to taste
½–1 tablespoon agave syrup

To make the noodle salad, rinse the kelp in fresh, clean cold water. Place in a bowl with the bell pepper, the chopped spring onions and the chopped marinated mushrooms. Season to taste. Mix through with your fingers and set aside.

To make the sweet-and-sour sauce, in a bowl, blend all the ingredients except for the agave syrup. Add just enough agave to sweeten the dish and adjust the seasoning.

Place a food form on each serving plate and build up a stack of the kelp mixture inside the form.

Trim the top off each tomato and carefully remove the flesh, leaving the shells intact. Fill with sweet-and-sour sauce and place to one side of the stack. Season with cracked pepper.

Serve with a green vegetable of your choice lightly drizzled with lime juice and oil.

Serves 2

Vegetable Coconut Curry

I am a great fan of curry flavours with my RAW vegetables. I mostly buy my powders ready mixed. Southern Indian flavours are aromatic, not so hot and work well with coconut and cashew milks. The tip is to let the curry sit for as long as you can so the natural flavours and aromatic qualities of the curry powder infuse the vegetables.

2 cups (12 oz/335 g) cauliflower florets
Salt and freshly ground black pepper, to taste
4 teaspoons lime juice
½ red bell pepper (capsicum), finely diced
½ zucchini (courgette), finely diced
½ carrot, finely diced
1 cup (6 oz/175 g) broccoli florets
½ celery stick, finely diced
1 small garlic clove, crushed

½ red chilli, finely chopped
1 teaspoon fresh root ginger, finely chopped
1½ tablespoons curry powder
1 teaspoon cumin powder
½ cup Cashew Nut Milk (see recipe) or use coconut milk for a sweeter taste
1 dessertspoon desiccated (dry unsweetened shredded) coconut
¼ cup fresh mint, shredded, to garnish

Put the cauliflower florets in a food processor and pulse until a rice-like consistency. Season with salt and half of the lime juice. Divide between two serving bowls.

Combine the bell pepper, zucchini, carrot, broccoli, celery, garlic, chilli, ginger, remaining lime juice, curry powder and cumin into a preparation bowl. Add the cashew nut milk and stir through the vegetables. The curry powder will begin to discolour the milk. Season to taste and set aside for a few hours.

Divide the curried vegetables between the serving bowls. Top with desiccated coconut and mint.

Serves 2

Spicy Vegetable Wraps with Sweet-and-Sour Dipping Sauce

Wraps are a great way to bring vegetable flavours together. They can also be great fun for kids if they get to make them up themselves.

1 choko or zucchini (courgette), julienned and soaked in lime juice
½ red bell pepper (capsicum), diced
2 spring onions (scallions), peeled and diced
½ small cucumber, diced
2 medium tomatoes, diced
½ kaffir lime leaf, vein removed, and leaf finely chopped
2 tablespoons lime juice
Salt and freshly ground black pepper, to taste
Green leaves such as lettuce, spinach, kale, collard or Chinese cabbage (choose leaves without too mnay veins)

FOR THE SWEET-AND-SOUR DIPPING SAUCE
1 garlic clove, crushed
¼ in/0.5 cm fresh ginger
¼ cup (2 fl oz/60 ml) macadamia oil
⅛ cup (1 fl oz/30 ml) Nama Shoyu (see introduction)
1 red chilli
2 teaspoons agave
Juice of 1–2 limes
Salt and freshly ground black pepper, to taste
¼ cup coriander (cilantro), chopped, to garnish

Combine the chokos or zucchini, shallots, cucumber, tomatoes, kaffir lime leaf, coriander and lime juice in a bowl. Mix to combine and season with salt and pepper. Set aside.

Remove the veins from the greens so that the leaves fold easily and begin to fill the leaves with diced vegetables from the end of the leaf closest to you. By doing it this way it will roll-up easily.

To make the sweet-and-sour dipping sauce, blend the ingredients in a blender until smooth. Taste and adjust the seasoning. Serve in small dipping dishes alongside the wraps. Garnish with coriander.

Serves 2

Pad Thai 'Noodles' with Peanut Sauce

This Asian-inspired favourite is one of a handful of oriental RAW food dishes that incorporate peanut sauce. RAW peanuts are rich in trace minerals and protein. Even salted ones are acceptable but, because they are roasted, there is not a great deal of nutrients left in them.

1 medium zucchini (courgette), peeled
1 red bell pepper (capsicum), finely sliced
1 medium red onion, diced
6 sugarsnap peas, chopped
¼ cup of basil, torn
¼ cup coriander (cilantro), finely chopped
2 teaspoons macadamia oil

FOR THE PEANUT SAUCE
1 cup (4 oz/115 g) RAW red peanuts, reduced to a
   paste in a blender

½ cup (4 fl oz/120 ml) cashew milk
⅓ cup (2½ fl oz/75 ml) namu shoyu sauce
1 teaspoon tamarind paste
1 red chilli
2 teaspoons fresh root ginger
2 teaspoons agave syrup
Freshly ground black pepper
2 teaspoons lime juice

Spiralise the zucchini to create noodles. Place with the rest of the chopped vegetables in a bowl. Add the basil and most of the coriander, retaining some for the garnish.

To make the peanut sauce, blend all the ingredients to a smooth, runny consistency, then pour over the vegetables. Thoroughly blend, then serve on individual plates garnished with coriander.

Serves 2

Tip: Remember to 'taste test' as you go.

Porcini and Cavolo Nero Risotto

This is one of my favourite dishes. It's an adaptation of a cooked version I saw in a magazine a few years ago. If you cannot find the dried porcini mushroom just use Swiss Brown or Portobello, both of which are freely available. However, the porcini imparts a lovely 'nutty-earthiness' flavour to the dish.

1 medium bunch of cavolo nero or kale, stripped of
    its veins
½ cup fresh or rehydrated porcini mushroom (soak for
    a few minutes in water until soft)

FOR THE CREAM SAUCE
1 cup (6 oz/175 g) RAW cashew nuts, soaked
    overnight in water
1 cup (8 fl oz/250 ml) water
1 garlic cloves, crushed
Juice of 1 lime
2 teaspoons olive oil

½ teaspoon desert salt
Freshly ground black pepper

FOR THE 'CHEESE'
3 white turnips, grated (shredded)
2 teaspoons nutritional (savoury) yeast
Freshly ground black pepper

FOR THE RICE
½ cauliflower
¼ cup (1¼ oz/35 g) pine nuts
1 garlic clove

To make the cream sauce, blend all of the ingredients together in a blender or food processor then set aside to allow the flavours to blend.

To make the cheese, in a bowl, mix the turnip with the nutritional (savoury) yeast. Season with pepper. Turn onto a baking sheet or teflex and dehydrate at 115°F (42.5°C) for 2–3 hours, or until separated and dried. Store in an airtight container once dried.

To make the rice, pulse all the ingredients together in a food processor. Use to cover the base of two medium soup plates.

Pour over the sauce so that it just covers the rice. Tear pieces of rinsed Cavolo Nero and scatter on top. Place the rehydrated porcini around the plate. Top with the 'turnip cheese'. Season with salt and pepper and finish with a drizzle of olive oil.

Serves 2

Veggie Patties with 'Spaghetti' and Tomato Sauce

This is a great family meal with plenty of flavour. The sweetness from the patties is combined with that of the tomato sauce and the 'pasta' like qualities of the zucchini. It's a treat for any night of the week.

FOR THE VEGGIE PATTIES
1 cup (4 oz/115 g) walnuts
1 cup (4 oz/115 g) almond flour (see introduction)
5 medium Portobello (Swiss brown) mushrooms
2 garlic cloves, crushed
½ red onion, diced
1 teaspoon mixed herbs
2 teaspoons fresh basil, torn
2 teaspoons olive oil, plus extra to drizzle
½ teaspoon salt
Freshly ground black pepper
½ cup Nut Parmesan Cheese (see recipe), plus extra
    to serve
Basil, to garnish

FOR THE SPAGHETTI
1 large zucchini (courgette), peeled
4 teaspoons lime juice

FOR THE TOMATO SAUCE
2 large tomatoes
½ red bell pepper (capsicum)
½ cup (3 oz/85 g) semi-dried tomatoes
1 large spring onion (scallion)
¼ garlic clove, crushed
¼ teaspoon dried herbs, or fresh basil, torn
2 teaspoons olive oil
4 teaspoons lime juice
1 teaspoon chives, finely diced
Salt and freshly ground black pepper, to taste

To make the veggie patties, blend all the ingredients except for the nut cheese in a food processor to a coarse consistency. Shape the mixture into patties approximately 1½ in (3 cm) diameter. Place on teflex or baking paper and dehydrate at 115°F (42.5°C) for 3–4 hours, or until the extrerior is crisp and firm.

Make the 'spaghetti' using a the large zucchini and the spiraliser. Add the lime juice and let sit for a few minutes.

To make the tomato sauce, blend all the ingredients until smooth in a blender or food processor.

Arrange a large food form on each serving plate and fill with zucchini. Place 3–4 veggie patties in the centre and pour over the tomato sauce. Top with some extra nut cheese, a small sprig of fresh basil, a drizzle with oil and a grind of black pepper.

Serves 2

Pea and Spinach Palak Tarts

In this recipe I have combined inspiration from India with Middle Eastern traditions. Palak paneer is a traditional Indian dish of cheese curds and spinach. I have added peas to the spinach part of the dish and combined it with dukkah. Dukkah is a Middle Eastern dish of mixed chopped nuts, dried herbs and spices. The dehydrated tart cases and the dukkah can be stored in airtight containers. Keep the dukkah in the refrigerator.

FOR THE TART BASE

1 cup (4¼ oz/115 g) sunflower seeds
½ cup (2½ oz/75 g) flaxseed meal (ground)
¼ cup (1 oz/30 g) psyllium husk
1 large garlic clove
1 teaspoon desert salt
1 cup (8 fl oz/250 ml) water
1 radish, sliced, to garnish

FOR THE PALAK FILLING

2 cups (9 oz/250 g) peas, fresh or frozen, thawed
1 cup (1½ oz/40 g) baby spinach leaves
1 garlic clove, crushed
¼ cup (1 oz/30 g) coriander (cilantro)
4 teaspoons macadamia oil
Salt and freshly ground black pepper, to taste

FOR THE CURRY DUKKAH

1 cup (4 oz/115 g) macadamia nut pieces
1 teaspoon curry powder

To make the tart base, in a food processor, blend all the dry ingredients to a fine powder. Add the water in small quantities to bring the mixture together to create a firm but moist dough. Push into the base and up the sides of mini tart tins (pans) to form the tart case

Place the tin on a tray in the dehydrator set at 115°F (42.5°C), or in a fan oven set to the lowest temperature for 4–5 hours, leaving the door open until the tarts are firm.

Carefully remove the case from the tins and place them directly onto the mesh in the dehydrator or onto baking paper for another few minutes to firm up the bases. Set aside. (These tarts may be stored in an airtight container for later use.)

To make the filling, blend all the Palak filling ingredients in a food processor. Ensure the mixture is not too wet, as this will make the tart base soggy. Turn the mix onto kitchen paper to soak up the excess moisture if it is soggy. Place a teaspoon into each tart case. Top each tart with a slice of red radish.

To make the curry dukkah, thoroughly mix the curry powder with the macadamia pieces. Sprinkle over the tarts just before serving.

Serves 2

Tamil Poriyal (Shredded Coconut, Carrot and Peas)

Looking for a colourful RAW food dish? This is a good choice. With its sweet and savoury combination, it can be served as a main meal or as a side dish to a vegetable curry.

4 carrots, cut into julienne strips
14 oz/400 g green beans, trimmed to $^3/8$ in (1 cm) pieces
2 cups (9 oz/250 g) fresh or frozen peas, thawed
1 cup (6 oz/175 g) fresh or dried coconut, shredded and soaked for 1–2 hours in cold water
2 teaspoons Curry Powder (see recipe)
Juice of 1 lime
4 teaspoons macadamia oil

Red chillies, sliced, to garnish
Salt and freshly ground black pepper, to taste

Add the beans and peas to a bowl with the coconut and curry powder. Blend together, then add the lime juice to create a moist mixture. Serve in a bowl, garnished with the red chillies.

Serves 2

Marrakesh Turnip Sticks and 'Midnight' Spice

I love exotic RAW dishes. In this dish I use the spice Ras el hanout (Arabic for 'head of the shop' meaning the top spice in the shop). Most ready mixed recipes include cardamom, nutmeg, anise, mace, cinnamon, ginger, peppers and turmeric.

2 medium white turnips, peeled and cut into
    matchstick lengths
6 cherry or grape tomatoes
1 medium white onion, diced
¼ cup fresh mint leaves, to garnish

FOR THE TOMATO SAUCE
2 large tomatoes
½ red bell pepper (capsicum)

½ cup (3 oz/85 g) semi-dried tomatoes
1 large spring onion (scallion)
2 garlic cloves
½ teaspoon ground cumin powder
¼ teaspoon Ras el hanout spice mix
2 teaspoons macadamia oil
4 teaspoons lime juice

Put the turnip sticks, tomato and onion in a bowl.

Put all the ingredients for the tomato sauce in a blender or processor and process until smooth and sauce-like. Pour over the vegetables and mix through. Turn onto a serving plate and garnish with the mint leaves.

Serves 2

South Indian Vegetable Sambar

Southern Indian dishes are less hot than those from the north, and have a sweet-freshness about them. A sambar is simply a vegetable stew.

Cauliflower, chopped into bite-size pieces
Broccoli, chopped into bite-size pieces
Zucchini (courgette) , chopped into bite-size pieces
Leeks, chopped into bite-size pieces
Tomato, chopped into bite-size pieces
Coriander (cilantro), to garnish

FOR THE SAUCE
12 fl oz/335 g can coconut cream or milk
1 in (2.5 cm) piece of fresh root ginger
Juice of 2 limes or lemons
2 teaspoons South Indian Sambar (see recipe)
1 teaspoon onion powder
1 teaspoon mustard powder
Salt and freshly ground black pepper, to taste

FOR THE SOUTH INDIAN SAMBAR
½ teaspoon coriander seeds
½ teaspoon besan flour
½ teaspoon cumin seeds
½ teaspoon black pepper
½ teaspoon mustard seed
½ teaspoon turmeric
½ teaspoon fenugreek seed
½ teaspoon amchur
½ teaspoon cinnamon powder
½ teaspoon dried curry leaves
¼ teaspoon mild chilli
¼ teaspoon asafoetida
¼ teaspoon salt

To make the South Indian Sambar, mix the ingredients together in a glass jar and shake to combine. Store sealed in the refrigerator.

Place the vegetables in a bowl.

To make the sauce, warm the can of coconut cream or milk in warm water or for 10 minutes in the dehydrator at 115°F (42.5°C) to melt the oils, which often aggregate in the bottom of the can. Shake the can before opening it.

Tip all the sauce ingredients into the bowl of a blender or food processor and blend to combine. Pour the sauce over the prepared vegetables. Leave to stand for a few hours so that the flavours meld.

Serves 2

Cauliflower Rice with Mint, Chilli and Lemon

Flavoursome cauliflower rice always goes down a treat. When I first began to serve my 'vege-rice' to unsuspecting guests, they were amazed at its freshness and taste. Cauliflower rice reacts beautifully to the introduction of fresh herbs and aromatic spices.

½ cauliflower
1 cup mint, coarsely chopped
1 red or green chilli
Juice of 1 large lemon
2 teaspoons macadamia or olive oil
Salt and freshly ground black pepper, to taste

Bell peppers, chives or red chillies, finely chopped, to garnish

Pulse all the ingredients together to create a 'rice-like' consistency, holding back some of the lemon juice. Garnish with the chopped vegetables or herbs. Grind some black pepper over the dish and add the remaining lemon juice.

Serves 2

Dolmades

I love dolmades, 'rice' wrapped in preserved vine/grape leaves. Vegetable rice is a great replacement for traditional rice when merged with the flavours of the Middle East cultures and is so easy to prepare.

1 vacuum pack of cured grape leaves.

FOR THE FILLING
¼ cup (1½ oz/45 g) olives, pitted and finely chopped
1 medium Portobello (Swiss brown) mushroom
¼ cup fresh dill, chopped
¼ cup (1¼ oz/40 g) raisins, soaked in water, chopped
1 teaspoon onion powder
¼ teaspoon freshly ground black pepper

1 garlic clove, crushed
¼ teaspoon mustard seed powder
Salt, to taste
1 cup (5 oz/150 g) cauliflower rice (florets pulsed to rice consistency)
2 teaspoons lemon or lime juice, plus extra for drizzling
1 tablespoon macadamia or olive oil, plus extra for drizzling

Soak the grape leaves in a bowl of warm water for 10 minutes to reduce the saltiness and to help separate the leaves. Strain and place on kitchen paper.

Lightly pulse all the filling ingredients to a 'rice size' consistency. Add lime juice and oil, then stir in the cauliflower rice. Taste and add more oil and lime juice, if required. The mixture should bind together but not be oily.

Open out the strained grape leaves. Set the stem-end facing you and place a dessertspoon of the filling above the stem. Trim off the stem.

Begin rolling, folding in the sides as you go until you have a neat dolmades parcel. Season with a splash of macadamia or olive oil along with a drizzle of lime or lemon juice.

Serves 2

Chickpea and Aubergine Moussaka

The key to this dish is thoroughly soaking the aubergine. Some of my RAW foodie friends leave theirs overnight so the 'meat' of the aubergine is thoroughly softened and sweeter to taste.

I large aubergine (eggplant), thinly sliced lengthways and soaked for 2 hours in salted water, then marinated in 1 cup (8 fl oz/250 ml) macadamia oil, ½ cup (4 fl oz/125 ml) apple cider vinegar and the juice from 2 lemons
1 cup (6oz/170g) sprouted chickpeas, pulsed to a thick consistency
Salt and freshly ground black pepper, to taste
Cinnamon, to garnish
Parsley, to garnish

FOR THE TOMATO SAUCE
3 large tomatoes
½ red bell pepper (capsicum)
½ cup (3 oz/85 g) semi-dried tomatoes
1 large spring onion (scallion)

2 garlic cloves, chopped finely
¼ teaspoon fresh or dried oregano
2 teaspoons macadamia oil
2 teaspoons lime juice
Salt and freshly ground black pepper, to taste

FOR THE CHEESY GARLIC CASHEW CREAM
1 cup (6 oz/175 g) RAW cashew nuts, soaked in water for 2–3 hours
1 garlic clove, crushed
¼ cup (2 fl oz/55 ml) cashew nut milk, coconut milk or coconut cream
2–4 teaspoons nutritional (savoury) yeast
2 teaspoons lime juice
Salt and freshly ground black pepper, to taste

To make the tomato sauce, blend all the ingredients in a blender set at half speed to a coarse-to-smooth consistency. Set aside.

To make the cheesy garlic cashew cream, blend all the ingredients together until smooth.

To assemble the moussaka, cover the base of a straight-sided baking dish with a layer of aubergine followed by a layer of the 'minced' chickpeas. Season with salt and pepper. Arrange another layer of aubergine on top followed by another layer of chickpeas.

Pour over the tomato sauce, followed by another layer of aubergine. Add a layer of cheesy garlic cashew cream to the top to about $3/8$ in (1 cm) thick. Dust cinnamon on top and season with pepper. Garnish with parsley.

Serves 2

Spinach and Nori Rolls with Wasabi Mayo

This is a RAW take on Japanese nori rolls. The Japanese classics adapt well to RAW food eating. These wraps will keep in an airtight container in the refrigerator for several days.

FOR THE OUTER WRAP

1 cup (1¼ oz/40 g) fresh spinach
1 cup (4½ oz/125 g) frozen peas, thawed
1 cup (8 oz/225 g) psyllium husks
½ cup (2½ oz/70 g) flaxseed meal (ground)
¼ cup (³/₁₆ oz/5 g) dulse seaweed flakes, soaked in water
1 garlic clove
1 teaspoon desert salt
1 cup (8 fl oz/250 ml) water, if required

FOR THE NORI ROLL

1 sheet nori seaweed paper
2 medium carrots, julienned
1 Lebanese cucumber, julienned
1 Japanese white radish, julienned
2 spring onions (scallions), trimmed to 2 in (5 cm) long
6 sprigs mesculin or mustard lettuce

FOR THE WASABI MAYO

1 cup (6 oz/175 g) cashew nuts, soaked overnight in water
1½–2 cups (12–16 fl oz/375–500 g) water
1 garlic clove
2 heaped teaspoons fresh wasabi (or equivalent from a tube)
Salt and freshly ground black pepper, to taste

To make the outer wrap, thoroughly blend all the ingredients in a food processor until a spongy consistency is achieved. The psyllium will soak up water and expand so add a little more water, if necessary.

Take a 'fist sized' amount of the mixture and spread onto a teflex sheet or baking paper to a square the same size as the nori sheet. Place in the dehydrator at 115°F (42.5°C) for 4 hours, or in a fan oven at 122°F (50°C) with the door ajar, for 2 hours. After 2 hours, turn the paper over and peel off the partially dried wrap. Never let the wraps get completely dry and crispy. Remove the wrap and trim the edges to the same width as the nori paper. Set aside.

To make the wasabi mayo, blend all the ingredients together, reserving some of the water, to make a thick but not too runny consistency. Taste and add more wasabi heat, if you like. Set aside in a serving bowl.

To assemble a nori roll, arrange a sushi mat on a clean work surface. Place the outer pre-dried wrap on the mat with a sheet of nori on top. On the end closest to you, arrange the carrot, cucumber, white radish, spring onion and the mesculin. Roll the wrap and nori paper around the vegetables, rolling the sushi mat around the wrap and away from you. Slice in half to serve and drizzle the wasabi mayo over the top.

Maki Sushi

This simple 'Maki Sushi' is my RAW food take on this traditional Japanese food. Include the tastes of Japan, pickled ginger, wasabi and shoyu sauce for an authentic taste.

½ cauliflower, broken into florets
2 teaspoons mirin
2 teaspoons rice wine vinegar
2 teaspoons lime juice
Shoyu sauce, to serve
Fresh wasabi, to serve
Pickled ginger, to serve

FOR THE SUSHI ROLLS
3 sheets of nori seaweed paper
2 carrots, cut into strips
1 Lebanese cucumber, cut into strips
1 avocado, cut into strips

To make the cauliflower rice, put the cauliflower in a food processor and pulse until just before rice consistency. Add the mirin, the rice wine vinegar and lime juice. Pulse again until the cauliflower has a rice-like consistency, without being wet and stodgy.

To make the sushi rolls, arrange a nori sheet on a sushi mat. Cover the sheet with ¼–3/8 in (0.5–1 cm) of the rice mixture leaving 3/8 in (1 cm) at the far edge.

Arrange the prepared vegetables and avocado across the edge closest to you. Pull up the mat to start the roll and, using a gentle but firm pressure, roll the rest of the sheet bringing the mat up and around the roll. Moisten the free edge at the top with water so it sticks to the rest of the roll.

Trim the ends to tidy them, then cut into 1½ in (4 cm) lengths. Serve with shoyu sauce, fresh wasabi and pickled ginger.

Daikon and Cabbage Kimchi Slaw

This is a 'quick kimchi'; the traditionally fermented Asian cabbage spiced with fish sauce. In this recipe I have introduced radish to give the salad a delightful peppery flavour.

½ Chinese cabbage
6 small red radishes
1 red onion
2 long white radishes (Japanese daikon radish is the best)
1 celery stick
1 red bell pepper (capsicum)
Juice of 4 limes

4 teaspoons macadamia oil
2 teaspoons rice wine vinegar
½ cup fresh coriander (cilantro), chopped
1 red chilli, plus extra to garnish
1 green chilli
1 in (2.5 cm) piece fresh root ginger, peeled
1 large garlic clove
Salt

In a food processor fitted with a shredder blade, shred the cabbage, radishes, onion, celery and bell pepper. Tip into a bowl and add the lime juice, oil and rice wine vinegar.

Replace the shredder on the food processor with a cutting blade and process the coriander, chillies, ginger and garlic and add to the other vegetables. Alternatively coarsely chop the ingredients.

Tip into a bowl, mix thoroughly with your hands, squeezing out the juices. Season with salt. Place in a serving dish and top with a red chilli garnish. Reserve the remaining juice to pour over salads or to drink.

Serves 2

Upside-Down 'Tuna' Sashimi

Using sunflower seeds to create a tuna-like taste and flavour experience is a staple technique in the RAW food world. Adding sweetness from a gherkin/pickle achieves this. The addition of the dulse seaweed adds a delightful 'fishiness' to the flavour.

4 large tomatoes, halved and seeds removed, cut into 'boat-like' strips

Dill, to garnish

FOR THE FILLING
1 cup (5 oz/150 g) sunflower seeds, soaked in water

1 large pickled gherkin, plus 2 teaspoons of the pickling liquid

¼ cup (2 fl oz/55 ml) lime or lemon juice

¼ teaspoon desert salt

½ white onion, finely chopped

¼ cup dill

½ cup (3 oz/85 g) celery, chopped

1 tablespoon rehydrated dulse seaweed flakes (soak in a glass of water for a few minutes)

To make the filling, pulse the seeds, gherkin, lime juice and salt in a food processor or blender until the seeds are completely broken down. Add the other ingredients, being careful not to over-process them.

Using a teaspoon, form small quenelles and place into the tomato 'boats'.

Serve on the platter. Add a small piece of dill as a garnish.

Serves 2

Green Tea 'No-Soba' Noodles with Dipping Sauce and Fresh Wasabi and Ginger

Traditional soba noodles are made from processed buckwheat noodles. I have replaced the processed noodle with zucchini noodles made using a spiraliser. The effect is the same but infinitely more nutritious.

4 zucchini (courgettes), peeled
2 teaspoons macadamia oil
¼ cup (4 oz/115 g) white sesame seeds
¼ teaspoon Matcha green tea or any concentrated green tea powder
¼ teaspoon desert salt
Juice of ½ lime
2 spring onions (scallions), thinly sliced on the diagonal
1 nori sheet, cut into strips
1 teaspoon dulse seaweed flakes, chopped

¼ in/0.5 cm fresh ginger, peeled and shredded, to serve
1 level teaspoon fresh wasabi paste, to serve

FOR THE DIPPING SAUCE
¼ cup (2 fl oz/55 ml) shoyu soy sauce
¼ cup (2 fl oz/55 ml) mirin
1 tablespoon rice wine vinegar
½ teaspoon coconut palm nectar crystals
Small piece finely chopped dulse seaweed flakes
1 small chilli, finely chopped

Spiralise the zucchini into a bowl. Add the macadamia oil, sesame seeds, green tea powder, salt and lime juice. Toss thoroughly and set aside.

To make the sauce, combine all the ingredients in a blender and set aside.

Divide the 'noodles' between the plates. Add the spring onions, top with nori strips and dulse flakes.

Serve the dipping sauce in a small bowl beside the noodles. Place the shredded ginger and the wasabi beside the noodles.

Serves 2

Sprouted Chickpea Falafel

There is something rustic about eating Middle Eastern street food with the hands. Preparing falafel which hasn't been deep fried is so refreshing – same taste and appearance surprisingly enough.

2 cups Cheesy Garlic Cashew Cream (see moussaka recipe), to serve
2 teaspoons lime or lemon juice
1 tablespoon coriander (cilantro), chopped

FOR THE FALAFEL
2 cups (1 lb 1 oz/475 g) dried chickpeas, soaked overnight and rinsed over 2–3 days to stimulate sprouting (see introduction)
1 cup (4½ oz/125 g) fresh or frozen peas, thawed
¼ red onion, diced

1 garlic clove
1 cup fresh coriander, finely chopped
½ teaspoon cumin powder
¼ teaspoon ground coriander
2 teaspoons lemon or lime juice
2 teaspoons macadamia or olive oil
Salt and freshly ground black pepper, to taste

Reserving some of the oil and juice, combine all the ingredients for the falafel in a food processor and blend thoroughly. The mixture should be a firm coarse consistency that you can roll into small patties.

Arrange the patties on the dehydrator drying tray, or in a baking dish if using a fan oven. Dehydrate at 115°F (42.5°C) for 3–4 hours, turning every hour. Alternately set the oven to 122°F (50°C), leaving the door open, and dry for 2–3 hours.

Mix the cheesy garlic cashew cream with the lemon juice and fresh coriander. Serve together on a plate as a starter or a main with a side salad.

Serves 2

Savoury Walnut 'Mince'

Once walnuts are soaked and turned into a 'mince' consistency, then topped with a beautifully rich tomato sauce, they have a meaty texture. The taste of this dish is crunchy, sweet and sublime. Serve with salads or used as a filler for peppers and avocados.

2 cups (7 oz/200 g) walnuts, soaked in water for a
    minimum of 2 hours
3–4 tomatoes
1 cup (6 oz/175 g) sun-dried or semi-dried tomatoes
2 tablespoons lime or lemon juice
1 tablespoon chilli powder
2 tablespoons cumin powder
2 tablespoons dried coriander or ½ cup fresh
    coriander (cilantro), finely chopped

2 tablespoons paprika
2 tablespoons garlic powder or 2 large garlic cloves,
    crushed
1 teaspoon oregano
2 teaspoons salt
Freshly ground black pepper

In a food processor, pulse the walnuts to a 'mince' consistency, then add the remaining ingredients and blend until combined. Spread the mixture out on teflex or baking paper and dehydrate for 4–6 hours at 115°F (42.5°C), stirring regularly. Do not over-dry; the best consistency is 'medium-chunky' and moist.

Serves 2

Stuffed Banana Peppers with Beans and Chickpeas

Red or yellow banana poeppers are long sweet peppers ideal for stuffing with your favourite vegetable combinations. Here is my 'take' using a fresh sprouted bean and chickpea filling. This filling also works well inside a tortilla.

2 banana peppers, sliced in half lengthwise with their
    seeds and 'strands' removed
Cashew Nut Cream (see recipe), mixed with
    4 teaspoons lemon juice, to serve
Chives, to serve
Spring onions (scallions), to serve

FOR THE BEAN FILLING
2 cups (1 lb 450 g) sprouted chickpeas or mung beans
11 oz/300 g fresh yellow butter (lima) beans, diced

1½ cups (8 oz/200 g) sunflower seeds (soaked)
¼ cup (2 fl oz/55 ml) olive oil
1 teaspoon shoyu sauce
½ red onion
¼ red chilli
1 garlic clove
1 teaspoon cumin powder
1 teaspoon nutritional (savoury) yeast
Salt and freshly ground black pepper, to taste

Using a food processor, blend all the bean filling ingredients to a 'rough to smooth' consistency, adding water as needed.

Spoon the mixture into the banana peppers and top with sour cream and chives or spring onions.

Serves 2

Veggie Stack with Ginger Sauce

If you are looking for some RAW food quickly, then this dish is for you. If you have remaining cashew nut cream or a garlic mayonnaise in your refrigerator, this will take just a few minutes to prepare. If you would like to make a sauce from scratch, I am sure you will like my suggestion.

2 medium carrots, julienned

Spring onions (scallions), finely sliced

Butter (lima) beans, washed

½ red bell pepper (capsicum)

1 zucchini (courgette), thinly sliced along the length

Olive oil, to drizzle

Freshly ground black pepper, to taste

FOR THE SAUCE

¼ white onion, chopped

½ cup (4 fl oz/125 ml) olive oil

2 teapsoons rice wine vinegar

1 in (2.5 cm) fresh ginger

1 zucchini (courgette), peeled

1 garlic clove

2 teaspoons shoyu namu

¼ cup (1½ oz/45 g) sun-dried tomatoes

4 medjool dates, pitted

Juice of 1 lime

½ teaspoon desert salt

Process all of the sauce ingredients together in a blender or processor until smooth and creamy. Taste and add extra seasoning, if needed.

Place 2 zucchini strips on a plate, arrange the carrots, spring onions, butter beans and bell pepper strips alongside. Pour some of the sauce over the top.

Place 2 more strips of zucchini on top of the sauce. Drizzle with olive oil and season with cracked pepper.

Serves 2

Squash and Zucchini Ribbons with Asian Greens and Mustard Mayo

RAW food is about using available vegetables and bringing in tastes and flavours. This is a wonderfully wholesome dish, which can be created for a simple dinner for two, or when you have numbers seated around your dining table.

2 yellow squash
2 medium zucchini (courgettes)
1 bok choy or similar Asian cabbage
½ red bell pepper (capsicum)
Juice of ½ lime
Olive oil, to drizzle
Freshly ground black pepper, to taste

FOR THE MUSTARD SAUCE
9 fl oz (250 ml) Garlic Cashew Cream (see recipe)
4 teaspoons olive oil
Freshly ground black pepper
Salt, to taste
Either 2 teaspoons mustard seed powder or 3
    teaspoons RAW Dijon mustard
½ cup (4 fl oz/125 ml) olive oil
1 teaspoon desert salt
⅓ cup (2 ½ fl oz/165 ml) apple cider or white wine
    vinegar

Using a mandolin, thinly slice the squash and the zucchini. Chop the bok choy into bite-size pieces. Slice the bell pepper into thin lengths. Drizzle with the lime juice and set aside for 2 hours so the lime infuses the squash and zucchini.

To make the mustard sauce, thoroughly blend all the ingredients in a blender. Add to the prepared vegetables and mix thoroughly. Turn out into a serving dish, drizzle with olive oil and a grind of pepper.

Serves 2

Tip: Check the label for Dijon mustard for non-RAW additives and preservatives. If you are making your own mustard, use a small blender.

Savoury Walnut 'Mince' with Zucchini, Mint and Peas

This recipe is about bringing flavours and textures together in one beautiful dish.

3 medium zucchini (courgettes)
2 cups (9 oz/250 g) fresh or frozen peas, thawed
2 medium tomatoes
½ cup fresh mint leaves
Juice of ½ lime
Salt and freshly ground black pepper, to taste
2 teaspoons olive oil, to drizzle

FOR THE SAVOURY WALNUT MINCE
2 cups (7 oz/200 g) walnuts, soaked in water for a minimum of 2 hours
3–4 tomatoes

1 cup (6 oz/175 g) sun-dried or semi-dried tomatoes
2 tablespoons lime or lemon juice
1 tablespoon chilli powder
2 tablespoons cumin powder
2 tablespoons dried coriander or ½ cup fresh coriander (cilantro), finely chopped
2 tablespoons paprika
2 tablespoons garlic powder or 2 large garlic cloves, crushed
1 teaspoon oregano
2 teaspoons salt
Freshly ground black pepper

In a food processor, pulse the walnuts to a 'mince' consistency. Add the remaining walnut mince ingredients then pulse the remaining ingredients into the mix.

To prepare the vegetables, peel the zucchini into strips and place on a flat serving dish. Spread the peas over the zucchini, then quarter the tomatoes lengthwise and arrange around the peas. Spread the savoury mince mix on top and finish by spreading the mint leaves around the dish. Add a final squeeze of lime juice and a grind of pepper.

Finish with a drizzle of olive oil.

Serves 2

Saffron 'Rice' Salad with Almonds

Using cauliflower or turnip as a rice alternative presents some wonderful opportunities to bring colour to the RAW table. The addition of saffron adds to the intensity of the colour of this dish and lends an earthy flavour.

4 threads dried saffron

4 teaspoons lemon juice

1½ cups (9 oz/250 g) cauliflower or turnip rice (see cauliflower rice recipe)

4 spring onions (scallions), finely chopped

1 Preserved Lemon (see recipe), finely chopped, or finely grated (shredded) zest of 1 lemon

⅓ cup (1½ oz/45 g) almonds, coarsely chopped and soaked in water for 12 hours

⅓ cup (3 fl oz/85 ml) lemon juice

⅓ cup (1¾ oz/50 g) fresh organic raisins

2 tablespoons fresh mint, shredded

¼ cup (1 oz/30 g) dried apricots, chopped and soaked in water for 2 hours

2 teaspoons orange zest, grated (shredded)

1 teaspoon ground coriander

1 teaspoon ground cumin

¼ cup (2 fl oz/55 g) macadamia or olive oil

Soak the saffron in the lemon juice in a small bowl for 2 hours so the colour is released from the stamen.

Pulse the cauliflower in a food processor until rice-like in consistency.

Turn the cauliflower rice into a large bowl and add the remaining ingredients including the saffron and lemon juice. Mix thoroughly so the saffron penetrates all the ingredients.

Serves 2

Fatoush

Fatoush is a classic Middle Eastern dish that is easy to make with easily accessible RAW ingredients. Use your Sunny Seed Bread as the alternative to the more usual fried pita bread.

6–8 Sunny Seed Bread snacks (see recipe)
6 cherry tomatoes, halved
1 red or Spanish (Bermuda) onion, roughly chopped
1 teaspoon sumac powder
1 Lebanese cucumber, roughly chopped
¾ cup mint leaves

1 cup parsley, roughly chopped
½ cup coriander (cilantro), roughly chopped
3 garlic cloves
3½ fl oz (100 ml) olive oil
Juice of 1 lemon
Salt and freshly ground black pepper, to taste

Place the cherry tomatoes, onion, cucumber, mint, parsley and coriander into a bowl. Sprinkle the sumac powder over these ingredients. Season with salt and pepper. Add the small bite-size pieces of seed bread to the salad and stir through.

In a mortar and pestle, grind the garlic with the salt into a fine paste. Then add lemon juice, olive oil and pepper. Adjust the seasoning to taste. Pour over the salad mixture and gently mix together.

Serves 2

Tip: If you do not have a mortar and pestle then use a small blender to blend spices. Leave to sit for a few minutes to allow the garlic and salt to infuse through the liquid before pouring over the salad.

Desserts

For many RAW food newbies desserts are often their first raw food eating experience. Usually these are fruit or nut-based desserts without any dairy or white refined sugar. Once you have made a few desserts you might like to 'strike out' and experiment with more complex recipes.

Chocolate Mousse

Rich, luxurious and 100 per cent 'guilt free', this RAW chocolate mousse takes moments to prepare and looks, feels and tastes delicious.

1 ripe avocado
1 ripe banana
2 teaspoons maple syrup or agave
2 teaspoons RAW cacao powder
½ teaspoon vanilla extract
Pinch of salt
Cacao nibs, to decorate

Place all the ingredients into a blender retaining a little agave and blitz until creamy and smooth.

Taste the dish and add the remaining agave if you want a sweeter dish. Spoon into serving glasses and top with cacao nibs.

Serves 2

Apple Pie with Pomegranate Cream

The RAW food version of a classic apple tart, this one has a rich nut case, filled with elegant slices of apple and topped with fruit.

¼ cup (1 oz/30 g) almonds, soaked for 12 hours in
  water and patted dry with kitchen paper.
7 Medjool or good quality Turkish dates, pit removed
1 teaspoon pomegranate syrup or juice from any
  freshly squeezed fruit, plus extra for drizzling
1 eating apple
¼ cup (2 fl oz/55 g) cashew milk

2 dessertspoons cashew paste (blend ½ cup (2 oz/
  60 g) of soaked cashews with a small amount of
  water to create a thick paste)
4 teaspoons agave syrup

To make the pie base, blend the almonds, dates and pomegranate syrup together in a blender. Pack the mixture into the base and up the sides of a small tart form and place in the freezer for 1 hour to firm up.

Peel and thinly slice the apple. Remove the base from the freezer and arrange the slices in a fan around the base. Place the tart on a serving plate.

In a separate bowl, add the cashew milk and the cashew paste together and hand whip into a thick creamy texture.

Drizzle some pomegranate syrup or remaining juice over the pie and around the plate.

Serves 2

Tip: Cut some of the apple peel into a 'twirl' and place on top of the pie.

Lime Pie with Berries

Lime pie is a much loved RAW food dessert that is often served in large slices in RAW food restaurants. I have scaled it down so that you can enjoy this sweet delicacy at home.

1–2 ripe avocados
Juice of 3 limes
4–6 teaspoons agave
1 teaspoon agar agar
½ cup (2 oz/75 g) fresh or thawed frozen berries of
    your choice

FOR THE BASE
½ cup (2½ oz/75 g) medjool dates, soaked in water for
    2 hours then finely chopped
½ cup (2 oz/60 g) almond meal (ground almonds)

Place a large food form on a white serving plate.

Place the soaked, chopped dates in bowl and mix with the almond meal and press into the base of the food form to the depth of ³/₈ in/1 cm. Set aside.

Now in a food processor, chop the avocado and mix with sufficient lime juice to taste, without making the mixture too acidic and wet. Add the agave and spoon in the agar agar. The secret is NOT to make the mixture too wet or it won't set. Spoon the mixture into the food form, filling to the edges and flatten the top.

Freeze for 1–2 hours, then leave at room temperature for 30 minutes. Run a knife around the edge of the form, right down to the base and gently lift over the top. Top with berries of your choice.

Serves 2

Orange and Carrot Sorbet

How do you know if an orange is sweet before cutting into it? Well if the little holes or 'pores' on the skin are close together and there are lots of them then the orange will be sweet. This dish is quirky and different and refreshingly sweet and cool on a hot summer's day.

1 large orange
1 medium carrot , peeled
Orange zest, to decorate
Pomegranate juice, to decorate

Peel the orange and the carrot and blend at full speed for 15 seconds. Tip out into cupcake moulds or a food form and freeze.

When you are ready to serve, simply run the back of the mould or sides of the form under warm water and tip out onto serving dishes. Be sure to not 'overheat' the mould otherwise the food will melt.

Decorate with orange zest or drizzle with pomegranate juice.

Serves 2

Sweet Pineapple, Cashew and Lime Sorbet

This naturally sweet and refreshing dish is a fabulous palate cleanser to eat after a spicy meal. With ginger, lime, pineapple and mint the flavours are intense.

½ fresh pineapple, diced and frozen for 24 hours
8 fresh limes, peeled and frozen for 24 hours
¼ cup (1½ oz/40 g) RAW cashew nuts
¼ teaspoon fresh root ginger
4 teaspoons agave
Mint leaves, to decorate

Blend all the ingredients in a blender or food processor until yogurt-like in consistency. Spoon into individual serving glasses and decorate with mint.

Serves 2

Muscat Brulée

The effect of the melted sugar on top of the sauce is quite stunning.

1 cup (90 g/3 ¼ oz) red and white seedless grapes,
   washed and marinated in ¼ cup (2 fl oz/55 g)
   muscat, sweet wine or liqueur for 12 hours.
2 teaspoons coconut palm nectar sugar

FOR THE SAUCE

1 cup (6 oz/175 g) cashew nuts, soaked in water for
   12 hours
1 cup (11 oz/300 g) coconut cream
¼ cup (2 fl oz/55 g) coconut oil, melted
½ teaspoon vanilla extract
2 teaspoons agave syrup

To make the sauce blend all of the ingredients together in a food processor or blender until smooth. Tip into a bowl and refrigerate to firm up. The coconut oil will cool down and bind the mixture together.

Divide the grapes between serving glasses. Spoon the sauce over the top and flatten with a spoon. Scatter over the coconut palm nectar sugar.

Use a chef's torch to melt the sugar or put the glass under a very hot grill (broiler) until the sugar caramelises. This might take just a few seconds.

Serves 2

Ryzogalo (Greek Rice Pudding)

Creamy textured RAW foods are comforting to eat. If hemp seeds are not available, pulse un-soaked almond kernels in a blender instead to create a savoury rice consistency.

2–3 cups (16–24 fl oz/500–750 ml) cashew or almond milk

2 cups (10 oz/280 g) hemp seeds or equivalent small almond pieces, soaked in water for 1 hour

½ cup (2 oz/60 g) macadamia nut pieces or finely crushed macadamia nuts

1 banana, mashed

4–5 tablespoons agave nectar

½ cup (2½ oz/75 g) raisins or sultanas (golden raisins), soaked

Cinnamon powder, to decorate

4 teaspoons agave, to decorate

Blueberries or any seasonal berries, to decorate

Mix all the ingredients except for the decorations in a mixing bowl until lightly blended, adding more or less nut milk to achieve a 'rice pudding' consistency. Tip into individual serving glasses.

Dust with cinnamon powder, a dash of agave and a berry, if desired.

Green Tea Cacao Sweets

Green tea powder has a strong flavour that can be used to impart a distinctive taste to desserts. Coconut adds sweetness to this dessert.

2 cups (8 oz/225 g) combined walnuts, pecans, pistachios or other nuts of your choice
6 fresh Medjool dates, pits removed and flesh chopped
2 teaspoons cacao powder
1 teaspoon vanilla extract
2 teaspoons Matcha green tea powder

4 teaspoons desiccated (dry unsweetened shredded) coconut (optional)

Combine the nuts and dates in a food processor until sticky, then add the cacao and vanilla and blend thoroughly.

Roll into bite-size balls and place on a serving dish. Dust with green tea powder, or roll in desiccated coconut.

Tip: Add a dash of agave or coconut palm nectar crystals for an extra sweet taste.

Raspberry Coconut Ice

These little frozen morsels can be served with chopped fruit, a strawberry coulis (puréed fresh strawberries) or any seasonal fruit.

1 cup (6 oz/175 g) cashew nuts, soaked in water for 12 hours then drained
1 cup (3 oz/85 g) fresh coconut or dessicated (dried shredded, unsweetened) coconut, soaked for 12 hours in water (then drained)
1 cup (11 oz/300 g) coconut cream
¼ cup (2 fl oz/60 ml) coconut oil

1 cup (6 oz/175 g) fresh or frozen raspberries
2 teaspoons coconut palm nectar sugar

Blend all the ingredients at high speed in a blender. Tip the mixture into a lined cake tin (pan). Tap the tin to level off and freeze for 20–30 minutes.

Turn out the frozen dessert (if the frozen mix doesn't drop out quickly run the based under warm water). Cut into squares, place in an airtight container and store in the refrigerator.

Pecan Bliss Balls

I love the sweetness of pecans. These nuts are rich in anti-oxidants and healthy fats. They are exceptionally good at regulating your 'elimination system'.

1 cup (4 oz/115 g) pecans
1 cup (5 oz/150 g) Medjool dates, pits removed
1 teaspoon vanilla extract
2 tablespoons cacao powder
4 teaspoons desiccated (dry unsweetened shredded)
    coconut, to decorate

Blend the pecans and dates in a food processor. Add the vanilla extract and cacao powder and blend until the ingredients are combined.

Roll a heaped teaspoon of the mixture between your palms into bite-sized balls then coat in desiccated coconut. They keep for weeks and are a great standby 'RAW sweet'.

Makes 12

Tip: Add raisins, dried apricots, pineapple or berries for variety in place of the dates.

Caramel Slice

Also know as 'millionaires' shortbread', this caramel slice is a popular RAW sweet dessert. A small slice of this has been known to send people into ecstasy. No dairy, wheat or sugar – pure guilt-free goodness.

FOR THE BASE
½ cup (2½ oz/75 g) Medjool dates, pits removed and flesh sliced
1½ cups (6 oz/175 g) RAW almonds (soaked, if you like)
1 teaspoon vanilla extract

FOR THE SAUCE
½ cup (4 fl oz/125 ml) tahini
½ cup (4 fl oz/125 ml) maple syrup
¼ cup (2 fl oz/55 ml) coconut oil, plus extra for greasing

1 teaspoon vanilla extract
Salt

FOR THE TOPPING
½ cup (4 fl oz/125 ml) coconut oil
4 tablespoons cacao powder
1 teaspoon carob powder
4 tablespoon coconut sugar or agave syrup
2 teaspoons coconut cream (optional but helps create a creamier texture)

Blend the dates and almonds together in a food processor until a fine to coarse consistency. Add the vanilla and mix again until combined.

Grease a rectangular dish with coconut oil, tip in the mixture and flatten, spreading it out to the sides to a depth of ¼ in (0.5 cm). Freeze for 1 hour or more.

To make the sauce, blend the ingredients in a bowl using a whisk and pour over the frozen base, ensuring it spreads out to the edges. Freeze to set, for about 20 minutes.

Meanwhile, to make the topping, melt the coconut oil until liquid over warm water or in the dehydrator. Add the remaining topping ingredients to the liquid and whisk to incorporate. Pour the topping over the caramel layer and smooth out to the edges. Freeze until set (about 1 hour). Turn out of the dish and cut into small squares to serve.

Makes 24 bite-size pieces or 16 larger pieces

Tip: Use plastic wrap (cling film) instead of coconut oil to to line the dish for a speedy and neat removal of the dessert.

Pistachio Cardamom Ice Cream

Frozen bananas make the most amazing RAW ice cream. In fact, they make a great base for any fruit ice cream. Freeze any gluts of soft fruits that you have, then blend them with banana to make beautiful fruit ice cream. For this recipe I have added some cardamom to pep up the flavour. This is a truly delectable dessert.

6–8 ripe bananas, frozen
½ cup (3½ oz/100 g) coconut palm nectar crystals
Seeds from 6 green cardamom pods (beans), cracked
1 teaspoon vanilla extract
1 cup (4 oz/115 g) pistachios, shelled but skins left on,
    plus a few extra to garnish
4 small fresh mint leaves, to decorate

At high speed blend the bananas to a yogurt-like consistency in a blender or food processor. Add the coconut palm nectar crystals. Tip into a mixing bowl and stir in the other ingredients.

Freeze for 20 minutes, then spoon into serving glasses. Garnish with left over crushed pistachios and top with a sprig of mint.

Serves 2

Tip: If you leave this mix for too long in the freezer it will become very hard and difficult to scoop out. I always make this dessert and eat it straightaway.

Aloe and Lime Granita

Limes are both refreshing and healthy taken either fresh or frozen. Aloe is high in vitamins and minerals. It has an alkaline-forming habit too so will help your body resist illness.

1 strip of aloe vera frond or 4 teaspoons
   unpasteurised bottled aloe juice
2 cups (16 fl oz/500 ml) lime juice (about 24 limes
   depending on their size)
6 teaspoons coconut palm nectar crystals
4 cups ice cubes
Zest of 1 lime, to decorate

2 shots tequila, to serve (optional)

To remove the content from the aloe leaf, using a knife, slit down the middle of the soft side and remove the green skin. Scoop out the clear gelatinous content and discard the leaf.

Place all the ingredients in a blender and at high speed, blitz until the ice breaks down to a smooth consistency. Divide between serving glasses and decorate with lime zest. Serve with a shot of tequila, if you like.

Preserved Lemons

Having some preserved lemons in a jar stashed in the store cupboard is a essential for me. These lemons are widely used in Middle Eastern dishes and are also perfect for adding to cauliflower rice or a basic green salad to add zest and a lovely salty flavour to the dish.

12 lemons
9 oz (250 g) desert salt
2 bay leaves
2 cinnamon sticks
Black pepper
2 cups (16 fl oz/475 ml) lemon juice
Olive oil

Cut a lemon into quarters making sure to not cut all the way through. Open up the lemon and fill the inside with a liberal quantity of salt. Place each lemon into a sterilised jar.

Add cinnamon, bay leaves and ground pepper. Pour over the lemon juice and top with $^3/_8$ in (1 cm) olive oil, ensuring the lemons are totally covered.

Seal the jar firmly and set aside. The lemons will be ready to eat in 6–8 weeks.

Index

First published in 2014 by
New Holland Publishers
London • Sydney • Cape Town • Auckland
www.newhollandpublishers.com • www.newholland.com.au

The Chandlery Unit 114 50 Westminster Bridge Road London SE1 7QY UK
1/66 Gibbes Street Chatswood NSW 2067 Australia
Wembley Square First Floor Solan Road Gardens Cape Town 8001 South Africa
218 Lake Road Northcote Auckland New Zealand

A catalogue record of this book is available at the British Library and at the National Library of Australia

ISBN: 9781742574882

10 9 8 7 6 5 4 3 2 1

Managing Director: Fiona Schultz
Publisher: Linda Williams
Editor: Simona Hill
Designer: Lorena Susak
Photographer: Phill Jackson
Stylist: Jaime Reyes
Production director: Olga Dementiev
Printer: Toppan Leefung Printing Limited

Follow New Holland Publishers on
Facebook: www.facebook.com/NewHollandPublishers